Law Essentials

HUMAN RIGHTS

T0333469

Law Essentials

HUMAN RIGHTS

Valerie Finch
Senior Lecturer in Law,
University of the West of Scotland

and

John McGroarty
Ph.D. student, The School of Law,
University of Glasgow

DUNDEE UNIVERSITY PRESS
2010

First edition published in Great Britain in 2010 by
Dundee University Press
University of Dundee
Dundee DD1 4HN

www.dundee.ac.uk/dup

ISBN 978 1 84586 057 8

No natural forests were destroyed to make this product; only farmed timber was used
and replanted.

British Library Cataloguing-in-Publication Data
A catalogue record for this book is available on request from the British Library

Typeset by Waverley Typesetters, Warham, Norfolk
Printed and bound by CPI Group (UK) Ltd, Croydon, CR0 4YY

CONTENTS

TABLE OF CASES

TABLE OF STATUTES

TABLE OF TREATIES AND CONVENTIONS

1 INTRODUCTION

This book is about human rights law as it applies in the domestic law of the United Kingdom. International human rights law has developed in importance over recent decades and it can now be said that human rights law is also an increasingly important element of the law of the United Kingdom. International human rights law is a very wide and complex area and so this book focuses mainly on the law which has developed as a result of the European Convention on Human Rights and Fundamental Freedoms of 1950. Human rights law has a particular significance in Scotland in the post-devolution era as Convention rights are binding upon the Scottish Parliament and the Scottish Executive.

THE EMERGENCE OF HUMAN RIGHTS LAW

During the 19th century a number of pacts and agreements were formed between western states. These were concerned for the most part with ensuring co-operation and peaceful relationships between the signatory states and had little to do with protecting the rights of individual citizens. There were of course some exceptions to this, the most notable being international conventions to abolish slavery. It was the two World Wars which were the catalyst for a move to protect the rights of ethnic minorities from which a wider human rights agenda gradually emerged. After the First World War, the League of Nations was established to promote international peace and security and guarantee the rights of ethnic minorities and the International Labour Organization was established to protect workers' rights. Unfortunately, during the period in which the League of Nations was trying to develop a spirit of co-operation between nations, several of the nations were more concerned with the doctrine of national sovereignty. In Europe, this was the era in which fascism and totalitarian principles of government were developing in several states. Germany withdrew from the league in 1933 and the League was not sufficiently influential to prevent the Second World War. It did, however establish a pattern for a permanent international organisation to promote peace and set a precedent for the establishment of the United Nations. The concept of internationally recognised freedoms was acknowledged in 1941, by President Roosevelt and Winston Churchill in the Atlantic Charter.

The aftermath of the Second World War, the Nazi holocaust and the horrors of these crimes against mankind led to the vast majority of the world community turning its attention to advancing the jurisprudence of what was then "humanitarian law". When the war ended, the victorious nations established the United Nations to promote peaceful relationships between states and as a safeguard against the recurrence of such atrocities. When it was established in 1945 the United Nations had 50 Member States. There are now nearly 200. Article 1 of the United Nations Charter states that one of the aims is "... promoting and encouraging respect for human rights and for fundamental freedoms for all". In order to achieve this purpose, the first few years after the war were devoted to the development of the Universal Declaration of Human Rights. This was adopted by the General Assembly of the United Nations in Paris in 1948 and the terminology "human rights" was adopted as a legal concept. This development at a global level was followed by the establishment of regional organisations with the aim of putting similar principles into a more local context. The Council of Europe was established in 1949 when the International Committee of the Movements of European Unity organised a Congress of Europe, in the Hague in 1949. Under the aegis of the Council of Europe, the European Convention for the Protection of Human Rights and Fundamental Freedoms was prepared for endorsement by states in 1950, and entered into force on 3 September 1953. There are similar regional Human Rights Conventions in other parts of the world, reflecting the principle that more stringent protection of individual human rights is possible among groups of states who have close affiliations.

SOME MILESTONES IN THE DEVELOPMENT OF HUMAN RIGHTS LAW

19th century	Agreements between Western states for co-operation and peaceful relationships – anti-slavery conventions.
1918	Establishment of League of Nations and the International Labour Organization
1933	Germany withdrew from the League of Nations
1941	Atlantic Charter
1945	Establishment of United Nations
1948	Universal Declaration of Human Rights
1949	Council of Europe was established
1950	The Convention for the Protection of Human Rights and Fundamental Freedoms was prepared for endorsement

1951	European Convention for the Protection of Human Rights and Fundamental Freedoms ratified by UK
1953	European Convention for the Protection of Human Rights and Fundamental Freedoms entered into force
1959	European Court of Human Rights established
1966	UK granted the right of individual petition to the ECHR (renewed every 5 years)
1969	Vienna Convention on the Law of Treaties agreed
1975	First judgment in a case against the UK: *Golder* v *United Kingdom* (1979–80)
1976	International Covenant on Civil and Political Rights and the International Covenant on Economic, Social and Cultural Rights entered into force
1980	Vienna Convention on the Law of Treaties entered into force
1998	Scotland Act
	Human Rights Act

INTERNATIONAL HUMAN RIGHTS LAW

The rules relating to international agreements were codified in the Vienna Convention on the Law of Treaties which was agreed in 1969 and entered into force in 1980. It is now generally accepted that international law will apply to a state regardless of its domestic law. Article 27 of the Vienna Convention provides that a state cannot plead conflict with its own domestic law as an excuse for contravention of international obligations. Another key aspect of the Vienna Convention is the procedure for entering into international agreements.

SUMMARY OF PROCEDURE FOR ENTERING INTO INTERNATIONAL AGREEMENTS

Negotiation

The terms of the international agreement are agreed by representatives of the original Member States.

Adoption

The agreement is adopted by the international organisation.

Ratification or signature

The Member States indicate their agreement to be bound. This may be by a formal signature or an indication by other means that they have ratified the agreement.

Entry into force

An international agreement usually enters into force once a specified number of Member States have ratified it.

Accession

Non-original states may accede to an existing international agreement by signature or ratification.

Amendments

The original agreement can be amended while it is in force. Amendments are agreed by negotiation between the Member States. Each amendment requires ratification by each Member State before it is binding on that state. (The Protocols to the ECHR are examples of such amendments.)

The agreement is binding on all Member States in international law

Each Member State may limit the extent to which it is bound by:

1 Reservation

Prior to ratification, a state may limit the extent to which it will be bound by specific provisions.

2 Derogations

Under some agreements Member States may derogate from certain obligations. This may be permitted without limit or for a fixed duration. Article 15 of the ECHR allows derogation from some obligations in time of war or public emergency.

3 Denunciation

A Member State may withdraw completely from all of its obligations under an international agreement.

The agreement may be binding in domestic law

Whether an international agreement is binding in the domestic law of a Member State depends on the Constitution of that state.

In some countries international law takes precedence over national law and international agreements are "self-executing" (USA, Germany, France) (monist approach).

In other countries international agreements are not incorporated into domestic law unless there is legislation which explicitly effects the incorporation (UK) (dualist approach).

Influence of international law on domestic law

In the absence of incorporation into UK law, the circumstances in which an international treaty should be taken into account are limited to the following categories.

Where legislation is ambiguous or the law is uncertain

In *R v Secretary of State for the Home Department, ex parte Brind* (1991) it was held that where a statute is clear and unambiguous, international principles and standards may not be relevant. However, regard ought to be had to treaties as an aid to interpretation. A presumption should be applied that Parliament must have intended to legislate in accordance with its international obligations. This case was an unsuccessful challenge to the decision to ban broadcasts by IRA figureheads which featured their own voices. A similar presumption was not accepted by the Scottish courts until 1996 when, in the case of *Re AMT (Known as AC)* (1996), Lord President Hope took the opportunity to clarify the extent to which regard should be given to the European Convention on Human Rights in Scots law. (This was before it was given further effect by the Scotland Act and the Human Rights Act.) The case was an appeal against a decision by the Lord Ordinary refusing to allow an adoption of a child by a homosexual man. It was held that when legislation is found to be ambiguous, Parliament is to be presumed to have legislated in conformity with the Convention and not in conflict with it. Lord Hope observed:

> "It is now an integral part of the general principles of European Community Law that fundamental human rights must be protected and that one of the sources to which regard may be made for an expression of rights is international treaties for the protection of rights on which Member States have collaborated or of which they are signatories."

Where legislation has been passed to bring the domestic law into line with the Convention

In the case of *R v Secretary of State for the Home Department, ex parte Norney* (1995) it was held that, where legislation has been passed with the specific purpose of securing conformity with international obligations in an aspect of domestic law, the court should have regard to the relevant international provisions. The case involved referral of prisoners serving life sentences to the parole board. In considering the exercise of the discretion to refer prisoners by a government minister it would be perverse to ignore the relevant provisions of the Convention.

Where administrative decisions affect fundamental rights

Where administrators are making decisions affecting fundamental rights and freedoms of individuals, it has been held that treaties such as the European Convention on Human Rights are a relevant consideration which the administrator should take into account before making a decision. A key authority for this principle is the case of *R* v *Ministry of Defence, ex parte Smith* (1996). In *R* v *Horseferry Road Magistrates' Court, ex parte Bennet* (1994) it was held that this did not mean that public authorities are bound to exercise their discretion consistently with the Convention, only that the procedures followed should show that the Convention rights have been taken into consideration.

THE COUNCIL OF EUROPE

Established in 1949, the Council of Europe aims to enhance, throughout Europe, universal and democratic values based on the Convention and other texts in relation to the protection and promotion of individual human rights and civil liberties. It has 47 members; the official languages are English and French, with the working languages of Russian, Italian and German. The Council has five observers, The Holy See, USA, Canada and Japan. The present political mandate for the Council was defined by the third Summit of Heads of State and Government held in Warsaw in May 2005.

The main purpose of the Council – the protection of human rights and the rule of law – is achieved via the promotion of constitutional and legislative reforms and the promotion of the concept of European public order. The Council seeks agreements on matters, which have occasionally been controversial, such as terrorism, trafficking, cloning and bioethics, cyber crime, violence against children, and xenophobia.

The three main organs of the Council of Europe are:

- Committee of Ministers, the council's main executive body;
- Parliamentary Assembly, with 636 members (318 representatives and 318 substitutes) from the states' 47 parliaments;
- Congress of Local and Regional Authorities composed of representatives of all the council's 47 local authorities and regions.

INTRODUCTION TO THE EUROPEAN COURT OF HUMAN RIGHTS

The key difference between many global international conventions and the European Convention on Human Rights is that it has an infrastructure for application and enforcement. Three institutions were given this responsibility:

- European Commission of Human Rights (set up in 1954);
- European Court of Human Rights (established in 1959 and then reconstituted in 1998);
- Committee of Ministers of the Council of Europe (ie the Ministers for Foreign Affairs of the Member States).

Prior to 1998, the Commission was responsible for conducting hearings to consider the admissibility of applications. As the volume of cases increased over the years, however, a huge backlog built up and a more streamlined procedure was called for. This was achieved by Protocol 11 to the Convention, which came into force in November 1998. Protocol 11 established a new single full-time court which takes all decisions on the admissibility and merits of applications. The Committee of Ministers is responsible for supervising the execution of the Court's Judgments but, since 1998, it takes no part in the proceedings of the Court.

THE NEW EUROPEAN COURT OF HUMAN RIGHTS

The Court, which sits in Strasbourg, is made up of judges nominated by each of the signatories of the European Convention on Human Rights. Not all the judges of the Court have been judges in their respective states; a significant proportion served as law professors, the remainder being former civil servants, politicians, and diplomats. Judges are elected by the Parliamentary Assembly of the Council of Europe for a term of 6 years. Judges sit as individuals. They do not represent their state.

Judges can sit in:

- Committees comprising two judges;
- Chambers comprising seven judges; and
- Grand Chamber comprising 17 judges.

Procedures for bringing a claim

Right to bring a claim

Three categories of distinct legal personality may raise actions on grounds of alleged breaches of the European Convention:

1 **High contracting parties**. These are the states which have ratified the Convention. A state may bring an action against another state, the inter-state application.

2 **Citizens of high contracting parties**. A person who believes that his rights under the Convention have been breached, may take a case against the government to the Court once all domestic routes are fully exhausted.

3 **Every natural or legal person**. Although the Convention rights are aimed primarily at the protection of the rights of people, there are some instances where an artificial legal person such as a corporation may have a right of action. An example of this would be that, under Art 1 of the first Protocol, a corporation may make a claim in relation to property under the Convention.

Complaints between high contracting parties were more common in the early years after the Convention was established. Currently the Court is concerned more with justice between individual citizens and alleged breaches of the Convention by the public authorities of the state in which they reside.

All domestic remedies must have been exhausted

All available remedies under domestic law must have been exhausted before a claim can be made (Art 35). This means that an individual may only lodge an application when there is no further court of appeal or where an appeal is certain to fail.

Time limit

The application must be registered within 6 months of the final decision of the highest court which had jurisdiction in the Member State.

Preliminary examination by a judge rapporteur

The rapporteur may refer a matter directly to a chamber if it is clear that it is admissible or to a Committee of three judges to determine whether the claim is admissible.

Admissibility stage

The committee of three judges considering the case at the admissibility stage always includes the national judge of the country alleged to be breaching the Convention. When applications go to the committee of three judges, only a unanimous decision will lead to the application being declared inadmissible; if the committee is unable to do this, the matter is referred to the Chamber.

The Chamber can make a decision on the admissibility and merits of an application. State applications go directly to the Chamber.

The criteria for admissibility are as follows:

- The matter must not have been investigated and ruled on previously.
- The matter must relate to a right protected by the Convention.
- There must be no relevant derogations or reservations in relation to that right by the state concerned.
- The application must relate to an organisation for which a Member State has responsibility.
- The application must not be an attack on another person's rights (Art 17).
- It must be genuine and based on good evidence of violation.

Merits stage

Decisions are made based on a simple majority whether the case is heard by a Chamber or a Grand Chamber (17 judges). At any time the Chamber may remit a case to a Grand Chamber if the case gives rise to a serious question of interpretation of the European Convention on Human Rights or where there is a possibility of departing from existing case law. The European Court of Human Rights, unlike our domestic courts, is not bound by *stare decisis* (legal precedent) in deciding cases before it, although it has been described as operating a "moderated doctrine of precedent". A judgment of a Chamber (seven judges), will be binding on the respondent state only after the expiry of a 3-month period, during which the state may request the case be referred to the Grand Chamber (17 judges).

Friendly settlement

A case may be terminated by a friendly settlement between the parties at any stage of the proceedings.

Pilot judgments

Due to the backlog of cases and the repetition of applications alleging breach of Convention rights, the Court has introduced pilot judgments to deal with systemic issues of breaches by a state, eg excessively long delays in pre-trial procedures in Turkey and Italy.

SUMMARY OF PROCEDURE

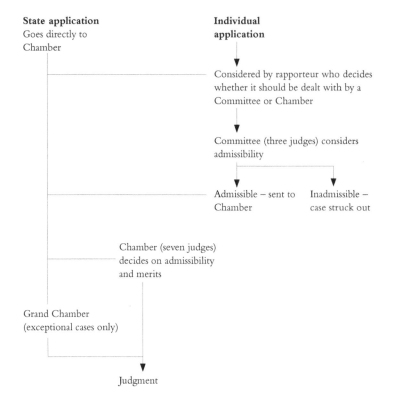

State application
Goes directly to
Chamber

**Individual
application**

Considered by rapporteur who decides
whether it should be dealt with by a
Committee or Chamber

Committee (three judges) considers
admissibility

Admissible – sent to　　　Inadmissible –
Chamber　　　　　　　　　case struck out

Chamber (seven judges)
decides on admissibility
and merits

Grand Chamber
(exceptional cases only)

Judgment

THE STRUCTURE OF THE CONVENTION

The European Convention on Human Rights is divided into Articles and
the Council of Europe has agreed and added Protocols to the Convention.
Some Protocols relate to procedural issues, whereas others guarantee rights
in addition to those included in the Convention. Articles 2–14 set out the
rights that are protected by the Convention. The United Kingdom has not
signed up to all of the Protocols that guarantee additional rights.

The Convention can be divided into three sections, each with
associated Protocols.

Section	Protocols
Section 1	
Articles 1–18	Protocols 1, 4, 6, 7, 12, 13
The rights and freedoms	Additional rights and freedoms

Section	Protocols
Section 2 Articles 19–51 Establishment of the European Court of Human Rights	Protocols 11, 14 Restructuring the organisation Amending procedures
Section 3 Articles 52–59 Miscellaneous provisions, including procedures for reservations, ratification and derogation	Protocols 2, 3, 5, 8, 9, 10 (*All now defunct – included in the main Articles of Protocol 11*)

STATUS OF PROTOCOLS IN THE UK

Protocol		UK status
1	1 Right to peaceful enjoyment of possessions 2 Right to education 3 Right to free elections	Ratified Ratified (reservation) Ratified
4	1 Prohibition of imprisonment for debt 2 Freedom of movement 3 Prohibition of expulsion of nationals 4 Prohibition of collective expulsion of aliens	Signed Signed Signed Signed
6	Abolition of the death penalty	Ratified
7	1 Procedural safeguards relating to the expulsion of aliens 2 Right of appeal in criminal matters 3 Compensation for wrongful conviction 4 Right not to be tried or punished twice 5 Equality between spouses	Not signed Not signed Not signed Not signed Not signed
11	Restructuring the organisation	Ratified
12	General prohibition of discrimination	Not signed
13	Complete abolition of the death penalty	Ratified
14	Amendments to the control system of the Convention	Ratified

Article 1   Responsibility of the state

The High Contracting Parties (ie the states) shall secure to everyone within jurisdiction the rights and freedoms defined in the Convention.

Article 1 therefore imposes a duty on each state to refrain from infringing the human rights of those within its jurisdiction. It also imposes an obligation on the state to protect people within its jurisdiction from suffering from breaches of their human rights. Any action against a state before the European Court of Human Rights is brought on the ground that the state has failed to fulfil this obligation.

Articles dealing with substantive rights

Article 2   Right to life

"1 Everyone's right to life shall be protected by law. No one shall be deprived of his life intentionally save in the execution of a sentence of a court following his conviction of a crime for which this penalty is provided by law.

2 Deprivation of life shall not be regarded as inflicted in contravention of this Article when it results from the use of force which is no more than absolutely necessary:

(a) in defence of any person from unlawful violence;

(b) in order to effect a lawful arrest or to prevent the escape of a person lawfully detained;

(c) in action lawfully taken for the purpose of quelling a riot or insurrection.

Article 3   Prohibition of torture

"No one shall be subject to torture or to inhuman or degrading treatment or punishment."

Article 4   Prohibition of slavery and forced labour.

"1 No one shall be held in slavery or servitude.

2 No one shall be required to perform forced or compulsory labour.

3 For the purpose of this Article the term "forced or compulsory labour" shall not include:

(a) any work required to be done in the ordinary course of detention imposed according to the provisions of Article 5 of this Convention or during conditional release from such detention;

(b) any service of military character or, in case of conscientious objectors in countries where they are recognised, service exacted instead of compulsory military service;

(c) any service exacted in case of emergency or calamity threatening the life or well-being of the community;

(d) any work or service which forms part of normal civic obligations."

Article 5 Right to liberty and security.

"1 Everyone has the right to liberty and security of person. No one shall be deprived of his liberty save in the following cases and in accordance with a procedure prescribed by law:

(a) the lawful detention of a person after conviction by a competent court;

(b) the lawful arrest or detention of a person for non-compliance with the lawful order of a court or in order to secure the fulfilment of any obligation prescribed by law;

(c) the lawful arrest or detention of a person effected for the purpose of bringing him before the competent legal authority on reasonable suspicion of having committed an offence or when it is reasonably considered necessary to prevent his committing an offence or fleeing after having done so;

(d) the detention of a minor by lawful order for the purpose of educational supervision or his lawful detention for the purpose of bringing him before the competent legal authority;

(e) the lawful detention of persons for the prevention of the spreading of infectious diseases, of persons of unsound mind, alcoholics, drug addicts or vagrants;

(f) the lawful arrest or detention of a person to prevent his effecting an unauthorised entry into the country or of a person against whom action is being taken with a view to deportation or extradition.

2 Everyone who is arrested shall be informed promptly, in a language which he understands, of the reasons for his arrest and any charges against him.

3 Everyone arrested or detained [on suspicion of having committed a crime] shall be brought promptly before a judge or other officer authorised by law to exercise judicial power and shall be entitled to trial within a reasonable time or to release pending trial. Release may be conditioned by guarantees to appear for trial.

4 Everyone who is deprived of liberty by arrest or detention shall be entitled to take proceedings by which the lawfulness of his detention shall be decided speedily by a court and his release ordered if the detention is not lawful.

5 Everyone who has been the victim of arrest or detention in contravention of the provisions of this Article shall have an enforceable right to compensation."

Article 6   Right to a fair trial

"1 In the determination of his civil rights and obligations and of any criminal charge against him, everyone is entitled to a fair and public hearing within a reasonable time by an independent and impartial tribunal established by law. Judgment shall be pronounced publicly but the press and public may be excluded from all or part of the trial in the interests of morals, public order or national security in a democratic society, where the interests of juveniles or the protection of the private life of the parties so require, or to the extent strictly necessary in the opinion of the court in special circumstances where publicity would prejudice the interests of justice.

2 Everyone charged with a criminal offence shall be presumed innocent until proved guilty according to law.

3 Everyone charged with a criminal offence has the following minimum rights:

(a) to be informed promptly, in a language which he understands and in detail, of the nature and cause of the accusation against him;

(b) to have adequate time and facilities for the preparation of his defence;

(c) to defend himself in person or through legal assistance of his own choosing or, if he has not sufficient means to pay for legal assistance, to be given it free when the interests of justice so require;

(d) to examine or have examined witnesses against him and to obtain the attendance and examination of witnesses on his behalf under the same conditions as witnesses against him;

(e) to have the free assistance of an interpreter if he cannot understand or speak the language used in court."

Article 7 Freedom from retroactive criminal convictions or penalties

"1 No one shall be held guilty of an offence on account of any act or omission which did not constitute a criminal offence under national or international law at the time when it was committed. Nor shall a heavier penalty be imposed than the one that was applicable at the time the criminal offence was committed.

2 This Article shall not prejudice the trial and punishment of any person for any act or omission which, at the time when it was committed, was criminal according to the general principles of law recognised by civilised nations."

Article 8 Right to respect for private and family life, one's home and correspondence

"1 Everyone has the right to respect for his private and family life, his home and his correspondence.

2 There shall be no interference by a public authority with the exercise of this right except such as is in accordance with the law and is necessary in a democratic society in the interests of national security, public safety or the economic well-being of the country, for the prevention of disorder or crime, for the protection of health or morals, or for the protection of the rights and freedoms of others."

Article 9 Freedom of thought, conscience and religion

"1 Everyone has the right to freedom of thought, conscience and religion; this right includes freedom to change his religion or belief and freedom, either alone or in community with others and in public or private, to manifest his religion and belief, in worship, teaching, practice and observance.

2 Freedom to manifest one's religion or beliefs shall be subject only to such limitations as are prescribed by law and are necessary in a democratic society in the interests of public safety, for the protection of public order, health or morals, or for the protection of the rights and freedoms of others."

Article 10 Freedom of expression

"1 Everyone has the right to freedom of expression. This right shall include freedom to hold opinions and to receive and impart information and ideas without interference by public authority and regardless of frontiers. This Article shall not prevent States from requiring the licensing of broadcasting, television or cinema enterprises.

2 The exercise of these freedoms, since it carries with it duties and responsibilities, may be subject to such formalities, conditions, restrictions or penalties as are prescribed by law and are necessary in a democratic society, in the interests of national security, territorial integrity or public safety, for the prevention of disorder or crime, for the protection of health or morals, for the protection of the reputation or rights of others, for preventing the disclosure of information received in confidence, or for maintaining the authority and impartiality of the judiciary.

Article 11   Freedom of assembly and association

"1 Everyone has the right to freedom of peaceful assembly and to freedom of association with others, including the right to form and join trade unions for the protection of his interests.

2 No restrictions shall be placed on the exercise of these rights other than such as are prescribed by law and are necessary in a democratic society in the interests of national security or public safety, for the prevention of disorder or crime, for the protection of health or morals, for the protection of the rights and freedoms of others. This Article shall not prevent the imposition of lawful restrictions on the exercise of these rights by members of the armed forces, of the police or of the administration of the State."

Article 12   Right to marry and found a family

"Men and women of marriageable age have the right to marry and to found a family, according to the national laws governing the exercise of this right."

Article 13   Right to an effective remedy

An effective remedy before a national authority must be secured to those whose rights and freedoms as set forth in the Convention have been violated.

Article 14   Prohibition of discrimination

"The enjoyment of rights and freedoms set forth in this Convention shall be secured without discrimination on any ground such as sex, race, colour, language, religion, political or other opinion, national or social origin, association with a national minority, property, birth or other status."

NB This is not a stand-alone right. It only protects against discrimination in relation to the other Convention rights.

The First Protocol

Article 1 Protection of property

"Every natural or legal person is entitled to the peaceful enjoyment of his possessions. No one shall be deprived of his possessions except in the public interest and subject to the conditions provided for by law and by the general principles of international law.

The preceding provisions shall not, however, in any way impair the right of a State to enforce such laws as it deems necessary to control the use of property in accordance with the general interest or to secure the payment of taxes or other contributions or penalties."

Article 2 Right to education

"No person shall be denied the right to education. In the exercise of any functions which it assumes in relation to education and to teaching, the State shall respect the right of parents to ensure such education and teaching in conformity with their own religious and philosophical convictions."

Article 3 Right to free elections

"The High Contracting Parties undertake to hold free elections at reasonable intervals by secret ballot, under conditions which will ensure the free expression of the opinion of the people in the choice of legislature."

HIERARCHY OF RIGHTS

There are three categories of rights that exist within the Convention:

- fundamental rights;
- procedural rights;
- qualified rights.

Fundamental rights (also referred to as absolute, unqualified rights)

Articles 2, 3, 4 and 7

A few Convention rights, such as the prohibition of slavery and the prohibition of torture, are absolute and subject to no possibility of derogation. They cannot be restricted and they are not balanced against any public interest arguments.

Procedural rights (also referred to as derogable, unqualified rights)

Articles 5 and 6

Rights such as the right to liberty and right to a fair hearing are limited only under explicit and finite circumstances defined in the Convention: eg a state may, under Art 15, derogate from the right to life in time of war or grave public emergency but only in respect of deaths resulting from lawful acts of war. *Lawless* v *Ireland* (1979–80) provides a suitable explanation of the "grave public emergency" criteria affecting the whole life of the nation.

Qualified rights

Articles 8–11

These are rights which are open to greater flexibility by the parties to the ECHR. For example, the right to respect for private and family life, one's home and correspondence, the right to freedom of thought, conscience and religion, to freedom of expression and to freedom of assembly and association all may be qualified, provided that the restrictions meet the following four criteria:

- they must be lawful;
- they must be intended to pursue a legitimate purpose;
- they must be "necessary in a democratic society"; and
- they must not be discriminatory.

| *Lawful restrictions* | Interference with Convention rights is prima facie unlawful; therefore any interference must be specifically authorised by an identifiable legal rule. |

Restrictions intended to pursue a legitimate purpose	Any interference with individual rights must have a legitimate objective. The relevant objectives are stated in each Article. In the case of *Handyside v United Kingdom* (1976) the Court was satisfied that, although the applicant's rights had been infringed, this was done for the legitimate purpose of the "protection of morals" of a child audience.
Necessity for the restriction	The restriction must not exceed that which is necessary to meet the stated legitimate purpose. According to the principle of proportionality, in order to be justified, the extent of the restriction must be sufficient to achieve its aim without restricting individual freedoms any more than is strictly necessary. The law should aim for a fair balance between the rights of individuals, and the needs of the wider community.
Restrictions must not be discriminatory	The Convention does not contain a general prohibition against discrimination *per se*. However, Art 14 prohibits discrimination in relation to the rights and freedoms in the Convention. Under the Convention, discrimination is established where a distinction in treatment has no reasonable and objective justification (*Belgian Linguistics* case (1968)). The concept of discrimination relates specifically to circumstances where restrictions that are reasonable when applied uniformly may be unreasonable if applied in a different way to different groups of people.

INTERPRETATIVE APPROACH TO THE ECHR

Introduction

It is important to remember that the European Convention on Human Rights is a treaty and that the European Court of Human Rights is an international tribunal which interprets the Treaty. In the *Belgian Linguistic* case (1979–80) the Court explained its operation in this way: "The Convention and the Protocol, which relate to matters normally falling within the domestic legal order of the Contracting States, are international instruments whose main purpose is to lay down certain international standards to be observed by the Contracting States in their relations with persons under their jurisdiction."

The Court is not a Court of "*quatrieme instance*" – that is to say, it is not a court of further appeal from national courts. It does not involve itself with the interpretation of the laws of the contracting state. It is concerned only with the question of whether the state has fulfilled its obligations under the Convention.

Principles of interpretation

Object and purpose of the Convention

Any interpretation of the terms of the Convention must give consideration to the object and purpose of the Convention. As it is first and foremost an instrument for the protection of individual human beings, its provisions should be interpreted so as to make its safeguards practical and effective (*Loizidou* v *Turkey* (1995)). This does not mean that there will be no restrictions whatsoever on individual rights or liberties since restrictions will often be justified. The legitimacy of each restriction on individual rights is considered on its own merits.

Uniform meaning for Convention terms

The Court of Human Rights interprets terms used in the Convention in a manner independent of their meaning under particular national laws. This is in order to secure consistent application regardless of the national legal systems from which a case originates. The terminology used under national law is taken into account for clarification.

Convention as a dynamic and evolving instrument

The Court of Human Rights has repeatedly stressed that the Convention is a living instrument which must be interpreted in the light of present-day conditions. This means that the original negotiations for the development of the Convention and the original statements of intent are rarely taken into account. As the Convention is a living instrument, the Court of Human Rights accepts that the effect of the Convention may change over time. The Court of Human Rights is aware of developing standards in human rights protection and its decisions take account of these changes in standards. This is especially evident in matters of a morality or sexual behaviour, eg changing attitudes to same-sex relationships, and transsexualism (*Goodwin* v *UK* (2002)). Academic criticism of the living instrument doctrine centres on it being judicial activism or policy-making by the judges of the European Court of Human Rights and exceeding their duties in interpreting the Convention.

Autonomous meaning

When a technical term is used in the Convention it does not necessarily have the same meaning as it would in any national legal system. The precise meaning of some terms may vary from state to state. For this reason the Court has developed its own set of definitions for a wide range of legal terms. This is known as the principle of autonomous meaning. It is important to be aware of this principle and not to assume that legal terms have the same meaning as they do in domestic law.

Margin of appreciation

When the European Court of Human Rights deliberates over an alleged breach of the ECHR it will allow the state, in certain circumstances, a margin of appreciation. The European Court of Human Rights recognises that state authorities are in a better position than the Court to assess what the interest of the society requires in their particular country. In the case of *Handyside* v *United Kingdom* (1979–80), the Court recognised the ability of the UK Government to assess the degree to which morality requires restrictions on obscene publications. It was stated in the judgement: "By reason of their direct and continuous contact with the vital forces of their countries, state authorities are, in principle, in a better position than the international judge to give an opinion on the exact content of those requirements ..." The margin of appreciation is a degree of deference accorded by the Court of Human Rights in recognition of the relative advantage of cultural awareness. This does not mean that states may take advantage to impose restrictions without limit. The restrictions have to be justified in each individual case before the Court. The attitude of the Court takes into account the context in which the restriction operates. A smaller margin of appreciation is allowed where the importance of the right at stake is greater. The Court also takes into account the particular purpose pursued by the state, and the degree to which practice varies among Convention states. A practical consequence of this is that there is a wider margin of appreciation for matters involving religious beliefs and cultural standards and a narrower margin of appreciation for matters such as the right to free elections. The operation of the margin of appreciation has the effect that cases from the European Court of Human Rights cannot all be regarded as of equal value when the courts in the United Kingdom are having regard to them. Cases which were brought against the United Kingdom will have the highest persuasive value. Thereafter, cases against other states in contexts where there is not a significant margin of appreciation will be more relevant than cases against other states in contexts where a wide margin of appreciation has been recognised.

THE POSITIVE OBLIGATIONS OF THE ECHR TO ITS SIGNATORIES

The Convention contains basic *minima* for protection of rights: it is a Convention and not a bill of rights; it is not merely preoccupied with victims being discriminated against and their rights under the ECHR being breached. Indeed, under certain circumstances states must take positive steps in all kinds of situations to promote the rights of citizens in the ECHR. Although the language of the ECHR is predominantly negative, many negative aspects in reality impose a positive obligation in the enjoyment of the right concerned, and are not simply obliging the signatories to refrain from the interference with the right concerned.

Examples of cases involving positive obligation include the following:

- *Right to life*　In a case where the allegation concerns a right and it is alleged it has been breached by the security services, forces or police, the state concerned is under a positive obligation to conduct a thorough, effective and impartial investigation into the complaint. (See *McCann, Farrell and Savage* v *United Kingdom* (1995); *Kaya* v *Turkey* (1999).)

- *Death threats*　In *Osman v United Kingdom* (2000) it was held that if there is an immediate and real risk to an individual's life or security, a state must take positive steps to protect that person.

- *Hospitals*　A positive obligation is found in that a hospital may have to consider the implications of Art 2 (the right to life), before refusing what may be termed life-saving treatment of a patient. (See *NHS Trust A* v *M* and *NHS Trust B* v *H* (2001).)

- *Vulnerable witnesses*　In *Baegen* v *Netherlands* (1995), the positive obligation of the state was extended to include that of vulnerable witnesses and victims of crime, especially in relation to the interpretation of Art 6, the right to a fair trial, and the rights of defendants in criminal proceedings: eg providing screens for certain types of witnesses, or giving evidence by video link outwith the courtroom.

Frequently Asked Questions

Is the European Convention on Human Rights part of European law?

This often causes confusion. The Council of Europe existed prior to the establishment of the European Union. It continues to exist as a separate (and larger) organisation. The European Convention on Human Rights is a treaty which was drawn up by the original members of the Council and which has been acceded to by other states. It is relevant to European law: for example, the Treaty of Amsterdam (Treaty on European Union 1997) stated that Community law is subject to the European Convention. There is a procedure to suspend some of the rights of the Member States and new states intending to join the European Union have to demonstrate commitment to individual rights before their membership will be considered.

Can a state withdraw from a treaty obligation?

It is possible for a state to withdraw from obligations under treaties. States often derogate from specific Articles but could withdraw completely from all obligations. This is known as denunciation and is rare. The United Kingdom has, on occasion derogated from obligations under Art 5 (the right to liberty). Derogations were in place during the troubles in Northern Ireland, permitting longer periods of pre-trial detention for suspected IRA terrorists. The implementation of the Terrorism Act 2000, as amended by the Terrorism Act 2006 which provides for longer periods of pre-trial detention of terrorist suspects, has required further derogations from Art 5.

Does the Human Rights Act protect people who are not resident in the UK but only visiting?

The wording of the Convention makes it clear that the state owes a duty to everyone within the jurisdiction. Even a person who is in the country as an illegal entrant and is awaiting deportation is entitled to challenge any infringement of their rights.

Essential Facts

- The European Convention on Human Rights (ECHR) is part of public international law; it is a Convention and *not* a bill of rights. It sets out the basic *minima* standards for the protection of rights.

- States are afforded, under certain circumstances, a margin of appreciation by the European Court of Human Rights. This is open to much academic criticism.
- There are three categories of rights under the ECHR: fundamental; procedural; qualified.
- Signatories to the ECHR may derogate from certain aspects of the ECHR, under certain provisions. The UK has, from 2000 onwards, in certain legislation, chosen to derogate from aspects of the ECHR, due to its claim of the threat from Islamic terrorism.
- The ECHR has "negative" and "positive" obligations on a state.
- The European Court of Human Rights is not an appellate court; it is not bound by *stare decisis*, but it does operate a "moderated doctrine of precedent".
- The European Court of Human Rights will only hear cases, brought by a "victim" alleging a "breach" of the ECHR, once all domestic remedies have been fully exhausted, or by one state to the ECHR against another state (inter-state application).
- The first case heard by the Court was *Lawless* v *Ireland* (1979–80).
- The first case heard by the Court concerning the UK was *Golder* v *United Kingdom* (1979–80).

Essential Cases

Ireland v United Kingdom (1979-80): Ireland brought a case to the European Court of Human Rights against the United Kingdom. The European Court of Human Rights held the breach was not torture, which was claimed by the Republic of Ireland, but inhuman and degrading treatment.

R v Secretary of State for the Home Department, ex parte Brind (1991): it was held that, where a statute is clear and unambiguous, international principles and standards may not be relevant.

Re AMT (Known as AC) (1996): when legislation is found to be ambiguous, Parliament is to be presumed to have legislated in conformity with a treaty and not in conflict with it.

R v Secretary of State for the Home Department, ex parte Norney (1995): where legislation has been passed with the specific purpose of securing conformity with international obligations, the court should have regard to those provisions.

Handyside v United Kingdom (1979–80): example of a legitimate purpose – the protection of morals – when banning obscene publications. Key case on the concept of margin of appreciation.

Baegen v Netherlands (1995): positive obligation to protect victims of crime and witnesses in criminal proceedings.

Osman v UK (2000) (the "death threat" case): states are under a positive obligation to protect individuals, under certain circumstances, if such lives are threatened.

2 SCOTS LAW AND HUMAN RIGHTS

Prior to the Scotland Act 1998 and the Human Rights Act 1998, if one considered oneself a victim, and that one's rights under the European Convention on Human Rights had been infringed in relation to a matter for which there was no remedy under domestic law, the only legal remedy was to apply to the European Court of Human Rights in Strasbourg. This often proved a lengthy and an expensive legal route. In the late 1990s, the Labour Party, while in opposition, conducted consultations as regards proposed human rights legislation for the UK. This became part of the Labour Party manifesto and, on taking office in 1997, the Labour Government published the White Paper *Bringing Rights Home*, which eventually led to the Human Rights Act 1998.

The Human Rights Act and the Scotland Act both received Royal Assent in November 1998, but the Scotland Act came into force one year earlier than the Human Rights Act. The two Acts complement one another in "giving further effect" to the European Convention on Human Rights in Scots law, and collectively enhance human rights jurisprudence in Scotland. The Scotland Act 1998 permits allegations of alleged breaches to be considered on executive acts from 20 May 1999, and breaches concerning the Acts of the Scottish Parliament from 1 July 1999. The Scotland Act permits the courts in Scotland to declare *ultra vires*, in whole or in part, Acts of the Scottish Parliament. This means that the European Convention has more constitutional significance in Scotland than the rest of the UK.

Since 2000, the Human Rights Act has been in force throughout the United Kingdom, giving further effect to the European Convention and allowing people to rely upon Convention rights directly in the UK courts. The option of legal redress via the Court in Strasbourg still exists, but only once the domestic legal routes have been fully exhausted. Private bodies and individuals are not required by the terms of the Human Rights Act to respect Convention rights, only public authorities; therefore, it is not possible to initiate court proceedings under the Human Rights Act against these.

SCOTLAND ACT 1998

The Scotland Act 1998 is the end process of a long period of political campaigning in Scotland for an assembly or parliament. Campaigners for devolution formed the Scottish Constitutional Convention (SCC) in 1988. The SCC produced a blueprint of aims advocating the "historic Scottish constitutional principle; that power is limited, should be dispersed and is derived from the people, not the sovereign" and to campaign for an assembly or a parliament for the Scots. There were further demands for devolution supported by the Labour and Liberal party in the 1980s and 1990s and, following the Labour Party's UK parliamentary general election victory in 1997, devolution in Scotland was achieved.

The Scotland Act begins with the sentence, "There shall be a Scottish Parliament". It encompasses much to do with the mechanics of a Scottish Government and Scottish Parliament but also contains some important provisions relating to human rights.

Challenges to the competence of an Act of the Scottish Parliament

Acts of the Scottish Parliament are invalid if they are incompatible with the Convention. Section 29 ordains that an Act of the Scottish Parliament is not law so far as any provision of the Act is outside the legislative competence of the Parliament. One of the factors which would cause an Act of the Scottish Parliament to be outside the legislative competence is if it is incompatible with any of the Convention rights.

Executive actions taken by public officials are also subject to challenge if they are incompatible with the Convention (ss 57 and 106). A member of the Scottish Executive has no power to make any subordinate legislation, or to do any other act, so far as the legislation or act is incompatible with any of the Convention rights or with Community law.

Exceptions to challenge include the following:

• The Lord Advocate in his role as head of the system of criminal prosecution.

• Where, as a result of provisions in primary legislation, the public authority could not have acted differently (Human Rights Act 1998, s 6(2)).

• The authority was acting to give effect to or enforce those provisions in or under primary legislation which cannot be read as compatible with Convention rights (Human Rights Act 1998, s 6(2)).

Questions about the legislative competence of a Bill or Act of the Scottish Parliament may arise in a number of different circumstances.

Challenge by individuals

Ordinary citizens who have been adversely affected by an Act which is in force may raise actions in the Court of Session. The most likely ground of challenge is that an Act is incompatible with the standards of the European Convention on Human Rights. Members of the public may not instigate a challenge to a Bill before it has been enacted. Only a person who has been directly affected as a "victim" will be able to challenge an Act. The procedure for challenge will be through judicial review procedure. (See *A (A Mental Patient)* v *Scottish Ministers* (2000).)

Challenge by Law Officers

One of the three Law Officers may challenge a Bill which he deems to be outside the legislative competence. If no agreement on amendments can be reached, the Bill would be referred to the Supreme Court prior to its receiving the Royal Assent (Scotland Act 1998, ss 32 and 33).

Under s 102 of the Scotland Act 1998, where any court or tribunal decides that:

(a) an Act of the Scottish Parliament or any provision of such an Act is not within the legislative competence of the Parliament, or

(b) a member of the Scottish Executive does not have the power to make, confirm or approve a provision of subordinate legislation that he has purported to make, confirm or approve,

the court or tribunal may make an order:

(a) Removing or limiting any retrospective effect of the decision, or

(b) Suspending the effect of the decision for any period and on any conditions to allow the defect to be corrected.

Examples of challenges to Acts of the Scottish Parliament

Examples of challenges to the Acts of the Scottish Parliament have included:

- Mental Health (Public Safety and Appeals) (Scotland) Act 1999;
- Protection of Wild Mammals (Scotland) Act 2002; and
- Convention Rights Compliance (Scotland) Act 2001.

Scottish Human Rights Commission

The Scottish Commission for Human Rights Act 2006 established an impartial, independent and statutory Scottish Human Rights

Commission, headed by a Commissioner. The Scottish Human Rights Commission aims to ensure that human rights are protected in Scotland via the development of a culture of human rights. The Scottish Human Rights Commission is independent of the Executive and reports to the Scottish Parliament. In the promotion of human rights, the Scottish Human Rights Commission aims to strengthen the culture, awareness and adoption of best practices of human rights in Scotland among public authorities.

The functions of the Commission include:

- monitoring and recommending changes to the law and to the policies and practices of public authorities;
- publishing information about human rights and providing advice and guidance;
- conducting research and providing education or training.

The Scottish Human Rights Commission has powers to:

- enter places of detention in connection with an inquiry;
- apply to intervene in civil cases in the Scottish courts, and to intervene in any other court or tribunal where the rules of that court or tribunal allow;
- conduct inquiries into Scottish public authorities in connection with general human rights matters;
- compel members of public authorities to give evidence or produce documents in relation to an inquiry.

NB   The Scottish Human Rights Commission does not have comparable powers to the English and Welsh equivalent, the Commission for Equality and Human Rights. The Scottish Human Rights Commission lacks the power to institute judicial review.

HUMAN RIGHTS ACT 1998

The fundamental principles of the Human Rights Act 1998 are as follows:

- legislation must be interpreted so as to comply with the Convention;
- courts and tribunals must take account of the jurisprudence of the European Court of Human Rights;

- public authorities must act in a manner compatible with Convention rights.

SUMMARY OF CONTENTS OF THE HUMAN RIGHTS ACT 1998

Overview	
Section 1	The Convention rights
Section 2	Interpretation of Convention rights
Legislation	
Section 3	Interpretation of legislation
Section 4	Declaration of incompatibility
Section 5	Right of Crown to intervene
Section 10	Power to take remedial action
Public authorities	
Section 6	Acts of public authorities
Section 7	Proceedings
Section 8	Remedies
Section 9	Judicial acts
Rights	
Section 11	Safeguard for existing human rights
Section 12	Freedom of expression
Section 13	Freedom of thought, conscience and religion
Derogations/Reservations	
Section 14	Derogations
Section 15	Reservations
Section 16	Period for which derogations have effect
Section 17	Review of derogations
Judges	
Section 18	Appointment of judges to European Court of Human Rights
Parliamentary procedure	
Section 19	Statements of compatibility
Section 20	Orders etc under this Act
Section 21	Interpretation etc
Section 22	Short title, commencement, extent

CHART ILLUSTRATING THE KEY CHANGES INTRODUCED BY THE
SCOTLAND ACT AND THE HUMAN RIGHTS ACT

Issue	Prior to 1999	After 2000
Statute incompatible with European Convention on Human Rights	Courts could not set it aside or question its validity	Declaration of incompatibility possible; or may be interpreted to render it compatible. *Westminster Statute – remains valid* *Act of the Scottish Parliament – may be declared invalid*
Delegated legislation incompatible with European Convention on Human Rights	Courts could only declare it invalid if it was *ultra vires* Courts could interpret it in a way which made it compatible	Courts can declare delegated legislation invalid, declare it incompatible or interpret it in a way which makes it compatible
Duty to decide a case on the basis of breach of Convention rights	No duty to do so	The courts must consider arguments based on breaches of Convention rights
Use of case law from the European Court of Human Rights in domestic courts	Courts may choose to consider as persuasive – in a few limited situations	Duty on courts to "have regard" to judgments from the European Court of Human Rights
Duty of courts in interpreting statutes	No specific duty to interpret so as to comply with European Convention on Human Rights	Duty to interpret statutes so far as is possible to comply with European Convention on Human Rights
Effect of actions by public authorities which breach Convention rights	Lawful (provided that convention rights were treated as a relevant consideration)	Unlawful and invalid.
Grounds for challenging actions of public authorities.	Only challengeable on grounds of illegality, irrationality or procedural impropriety	Can also be challenged on ground of lack of compliance with European Convention on Human Rights

Issue	Prior to 1999	After 2000
Remedies for breaches of Convention rights	Case may be taken to Strasbourg after all domestic remedies exhausted	Remedies are available in domestic courts; challenges may be made via judicial review procedure or a breach of Convention rights may be argued in defence in the course of any action
		Case may be taken to Strasbourg after all domestic remedies exhausted

KEY PROVISIONS OF THE HUMAN RIGHTS ACT 1998

Further effect for Convention rights

Section 1 defines the ECHR rights which are being given further effect by the Human Rights Act as follows:

- Arts 2–12 and 14 of the Convention;
- Arts 1–3 of the First Protocol;
- Arts 1–2 of the Sixth Protocol.

These are the sections which contain the substantive rights. The majority of the rest of the Articles are concerned with procedural matters which are not relevant to domestic law. There are, however, two Articles whose omission requires explanation. The first of these is Art 1 which provides that the state must secure to everyone the Convention rights. The view of the government was that it was not appropriate to incorporate a general international obligation of this nature into UK law. The whole of the Human Rights Act can be seen as a measure aimed at fulfilling this duty. If the human rights protection provided by domestic law is inadequate then the remedy is to take a case against the government to the European Court of Human Rights in Strasbourg.

The second missing Article is Art 13 which states that an effective remedy must be available to anyone whose Convention rights have been violated. The government's view of Art 13 was that it was not necessary as s 8 of the Human Rights Act lays down comprehensive remedies. Domestic courts may still have regard to European Court of Human Rights case law relating to Art 13, when considering remedies under s 8, even though they are not bound to do so. The key importance of Art 13 is not diminished by the fact that it is not included in the Human Rights Act. Along with Art 1 it provides the basis for any action against the state before the European Court of Human Rights in Strasbourg. The fundamental ground for any challenge is that a state has failed to provide adequate human rights protection (Art 1) and has failed to provide an adequate remedy (Art 13).

Taking case law of the European Court of Human Rights into account

A court or tribunal determining a question in connection with a Convention right must have regard to the relevant judgments, decisions, declarations and opinions of the European Commission and Court of Human Rights and the Committee of Ministers of the Council of Europe (s 2). The important point here is that this does not mean that the UK courts are bound by decisions from the European Court of Human Rights. The general principle that the United Kingdom is not bound in international law to follow European Court of Human Rights judgments in cases to which it is not a party still applies. Section 2 simply imposes a duty to have regard to the case law from Strasbourg. The persuasive value of a judgment will depend a number of factors.

FACTORS WHICH INFLUENCE THE PERSUASIVE VALUE OF JUDGMENTS
FROM THE EUROPEAN COURT OF HUMAN RIGHTS

Factor		Persuasive value
Was the UK Government a respondent in the case?	→ Yes	Higher
	→ No	Lower
Is the context of a case where the respondent is not the UK one in which a wide margin of appreciation exists?	→ Yes	Lower
	→ No	Higher
Is the judgment from • Commission prior to the changes to the European Court of Human Rights? • A Chamber or Grand Chamber?	→ Yes → Yes	Lower Higher
Is the judgment recent?	→ Yes	Higher
	→ No	Lower

The wording of the Act permits UK courts to depart from existing Strasbourg decisions where it is appropriate to do so.

Interpretation of legislation

All courts and tribunals shall give effect to legislation, so far as possible, consistently with the Convention rights (s 3). This principle applies to all domestic primary and secondary legislation. Legislation may be reinterpreted in order to render it compatible with the Convention. This is a major change from the position prior to the Human Rights Act 1998 when courts could only use the Convention to interpret legislation which was unclear or ambiguous. In the course of interpreting and applying legislation there will be a presumption that the intention was to legislate in a manner compatible with the Convention.

The Human Rights Act has not provided that Parliament must legislate in conformity with the Convention. Parliament is, however, required to give consideration to the Convention when preparing legislation. A Minister in charge of a Bill in the Westminster Parliament must make a written statement as to whether or not the provisions of the Bill are compatible with the Convention rights (s 19). If he is unable to make the statement of compatibility, he can state that, nevertheless, he wishes to proceed with the Bill. This ensures a focus at the earliest of legislative stages on compliance with human rights jurisprudence. It also leaves the doctrine of the supremacy of Parliament in place as Parliament can still choose to legislate in a way that infringes Convention rights and, in such a case, the courts will be obliged to uphold the legislation although a declaration of incompatibility could be issued.

Declaration of incompatibility

If a judge is convinced that primary unambiguous legislation is inconsistent with the Convention, he can make a declaration of incompatibility. This will draw the matter to the attention of Ministers and Parliament. The Courts which have this power in relation to Scotland are: the Supreme Court, the House of Lords, the Courts-Martial Appeal Court, the High Court of Justiciary sitting as a court of criminal appeal and the Court of Session (s 4(5)). The supremacy of Parliament will not be threatened by declarations of incompatibility since, theoretically at least, Parliament may ignore such declarations. Section 4(6) states that a declaration of incompatibility does not affect the validity or continuing operation of enforcement of the provision in respect of which it is being given. The Act also provides that the declaration is not binding on the parties to the proceedings in which it is made. A Minister of the Crown may, by a remedial order, make such amendments to the legislation as he considers appropriate (s 10).

NB This contrasts with the equivalent measures in the Scotland Act 1998, which provide that an Act of the Scottish Parliament can be declared invalid.

Declarations of incompatibility have been made in relation to the following:

- Mental Health Act 1983;
- Offences Against the Person Act 1861;
- the penalty scheme in the Immigration and Asylum Act 1999;
- Crime (Sentences) Act 1997;
- Human Fertilisation and Embryology Act 1990;
- Matrimonial Causes Act 1973;
- Social Security Contributions and Benefits Act 1992;
- Income and Corporation Taxes Act 1988;
- Human Rights Act (1998) (Designated Derogation) Order 2001;
- Housing Act 1996;
- Asylum and Immigration (Treatment of Claimants, etc) Act 2004.

A particularly interesting declaration of incompatibility arose in the case of *A* v *Secretary of State for the Home Department* (2004) (the *Belmarsh* case). The Appellate Committee of the House of Lords issued a declaration of incompatibility concerning the UK Government's right to detain foreign nationals on mere suspicion of a terrorist-related offence. The Appellate Committee declared that s 23 of the Anti-terrorism, Crime and Security Act 2001 was incompatible with the Art 5 right to liberty of the European Convention on Human Rights, on the ground that it is not proportionate, and that it is incompatible with Art 14 of the same Convention. This led to fresh legislative terrorism provisions: the Prevention of Terrorism Act 2005 and the introduction of control orders similar to the 2001 legislation that the Lords declared was incompatible with the Convention. The UK Government then secured a further derogation from the European Convention on Human Rights relating to provisions of the Prevention of Terrorism Act 2005. The UK Government claimed the derogations were necessary on grounds of national security and the threat from Islamic terrorism.

Remedial action

Section 10 provides fast-track procedures for amending legislation in two circumstances:

- where a declaration of incompatibility has been made;
- in response to a finding of the European Court of Human Rights.

The procedure can be used to make changes more quickly than the normal parliamentary process allows. A Minister can make a remedial order to amend the legislation. There are some conditions and safeguards to ensure that this procedure is not used as a way of achieving changes to legislation for other purposes:

- All routes of appeal must have been exhausted.
- There must be a compelling reason to amend the legislation.
- The power may only be used to remove incompatible provisions in legislation so as to protect human rights.★
- A draft of the order must be laid before Parliament with an explanation of the incompatibility and the reasons for proceeding under s 10.
- There are minimum periods for consultation.★

Activist or minimalist approach to interpretation

Arising from ss 3 and 4 are a number of cases which discuss when s 3 should be used to reinterpret a statute and when a declaration of incompatibility under s 4 should be made. Section 3 allows robust interpretation but there is a danger that judges may overstep the mark and rewrite legislation. Judicial activism is when judges adopt creative approaches to interpretation, for example by reading implied words into legislation. An example of this approach was in *R* v *A (No 2)* (2002): there was disagreement between Lord Steyn and Lord Hope on this matter. Lord Steyn noted, "[I]n accordance with the will of Parliament it will sometimes be necessary to adopt an interpretation which linguistically will appear strained ... A declaration of incompatibility is a measure of last resort and must be avoided unless it is plainly impossible to do so." Lord Hope disagreed, commenting that the rule of construction in s 3 of the Human Rights Act was "... only a rule of interpretation. It does not entitle the Judges to act as legislators ... the compatibility is to be achieved only so far as this is possible. Plainly this will not be possible if the legislation contains provisions which expressly

---

★ Note that, in exceptionally urgent cases, a Minister may be allowed to make the order prior to laying it before Parliament (Sch 2, para 2(b)).

contradict the meaning which the enactment would have to be given to make it compatible". According to Lord Hope, if a contradiction did exist, the issue of a declaration of incompatibility ought to be issued, and then it should be left to Parliament to decide whether to change the legislation.

The minimalist approach which was favoured by Lord Hope was exemplified by the case of *Brown* v *Stott* (2001) where the House of Lords considered whether s 172 of the Road Traffic Act 1998 was compatible with the right under Art 6 to a fair trial. Section 172 makes it an offence for motorists not to tell the police who was driving their vehicle when a traffic offence has been detected. The motorist's statement can be used as evidence in the trial for the offence in question. It was argued that this offended against the right not to incriminate oneself. The House of Lords ruled that s 172 was not incompatible with Art 6 as the freedom from self-incrimination was not an absolute right but was a right which should be balanced against the wider needs of society. It was stated in the judgment that deference should be shown by the courts to the discretion of the legislature.

PROCESS OF JUDICIAL DECISION–MAKING IN RELATION TO
INTERPRETATION OF LEGISLATION

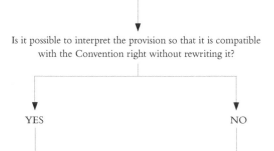

Legislation appears to be incompatible with a Convention right

Is it possible to interpret the provision so that it is compatible with the Convention right without rewriting it?

YES

NO

The court has a duty to read the legislation so the Convention rights are protected

The court can issue a declaration of incompatibility which remits the issue back to Parliament where the legislation can be reviewed

Acts of public authorities

All public authorities, including courts, are bound to act in a manner compatible with the Convention (s 6(1)). The term "public authority" includes all courts and tribunals and "any person certain of whose functions are functions of a public nature". This definition has proved difficult in practice. Where the functions of an organisation are only partly public in nature then it is only bound by s 6 in respect of its public functions. This wide definition of public authorities reaches private companies conducting government work and organisations such as utility companies: eg the Procurator Fiscal Service, the NHS, local government, police forces, Prison Service and the privatised utilities.

Organisations	Liability under the Human Rights Act 1998
Obvious public authorities, UK Government departments, Scottish Government departments, police forces	All acts are subject to liability under the Act
Hybrid organisations with a mix of public and private functions: eg the Law Society, BBC, private prison companies	Liable for their public acts but not their private acts
Organisations with no public functions	No liability

Section 6 does not provide a completely new remedy, but develops the circumstances in which judicial review is used by the courts. In *R (Daly)* v *Home Secretary* (2003), the House of Lords held that the Human Rights Act did not require courts to review the merits of administrative decisions. Courts should apply the legal test of "proportionality" which is a relatively new concept in the field of judicial review.

Defence of statutory authority

A public authority will *not* be deemed to have acted unlawfully under the Human Rights Act 1998 as a result of primary legislation (of the UK Parliament), if it could *not* have acted differently. In other words, the defence of statutory authority still exists; however, the courts will look with anxious scrutiny to see if the interference with the Convention right was necessary to achieve one or more of the Convention aims. Where statutory authority exists and the official could not have acted differently, the most the person can hope to achieve is a declaration of incompatibility.

Proceedings

An individual who claims that a public authority has acted or proposes to act in a way which is unlawful in terms of s 6 may bring proceedings against the public authority in the appropriate court or tribunal. The most appropriate court proceedings to bring against a public authority will be an application for judicial review. Judicial review is a procedure for exercising the common law supervisory jurisdiction of the Court of Session which has been recognised since 1532. Judicial review ensures that administrative and other bodies, as entrusted by Parliament, act within the law. It is not concerned with the merits of the decision or matter in question. Scots law does not limit the availability of a judicial review on a strict public/private law approach (*West* v *Secretary of State for Scotland* (1992)). Judicial review procedure can be used wherever a power or authority has been conferred on a person or organisation which affects the rights of a third person (a tripartite relationship). The consequences of the Human Rights Act 1998 and the Scotland Act 1998 are that the grounds for judicial review are no longer limited to questions of irrationality, illegality or procedural impropriety, as expounded by Lord Diplock in *Civil Service Unions* v *Minister for Civil Service* (1985), but are expanded to include compatibility with the European Convention on Human Rights. The Court of Session now considers, for example, whether an action has been proportionate in terms of the legitimate purpose to be achieved, balanced against the effect on the individual of the infringement of his rights.

A person may rely on the Convention right or rights in any legal proceedings against him (s 7). This may arise, for example, in the course of criminal proceedings when a defender may wish to argue that his Convention rights have been infringed. This occurred in the case of *Starrs* v *Ruxton* (2000) where a defender claimed that his right to a fair trial under Art 6 had been breached as the judge was a temporary sheriff and was therefore not sufficiently independent.

Victim test

A challenge may be brought only by a person who qualifies as a "victim" of a violation of a Convention right. This means he has to show that he has been or is likely to be affected directly by the breach of the Convention. The definition of a victim has been given a generous interpretation. In *Re S; Re W* (2002), Lord Nicholls of Birkenhead noted, of the Human Rights Act, "sections 7 and 8 are to be given generous interpretations, as befits their human rights purpose". This is always subject to the fact that the person(s) must be a victim(s), as in *Klass* v *Germany* (1979–80) where it was held that if an applicant is to be successful, before the European Court of Human Rights, he will have to be able to claim to have been affected by the violation he alleges. The Convention does not allow individuals to apply to the Court merely because they believe a particular law contravenes the Convention. The alleged breach of the

European Convention on Human Rights must have been, or be likely to be, a distinct disadvantage to the individual.

Three cases show wide interpretation of the victim test by the European Court of Human Rights:

- In *Sutherland* v *UK* (1997), a sexually active homosexual man was held to be entitled to complain to the European Court of Human Rights concerning the law in the UK relating to the age of consent for lawful homosexual intercourse. Although he had never been prosecuted, there was a possibility that he could be and so he could be classed as a victim.

- In *Campbell and Cosans* v *UK* (1982), children attending Scottish secondary schools where corporal punishment was practised were considered victims on the basis that they had "a direct an immediate interest in complaining" even though they had not in fact been punished.

- In *McCann, Farrell and Savage* v *UK* (1995), the relatives of IRA terrorists who had been shot dead by British forces in Gibraltar were allowed to bring a case to the European Court of Human Rights.

Time limit

Under s 7(5) proceedings must be brought against a public authority within 1 year; however, under s 7(5)(b), the court has a discretion to extend the period where it is equitable to do so. This rule is subject to any stricter time limits which were already in place: for example, many statutes specify a stricter time limit for challenges to decisions.

Remedies

The court or tribunal may grant such relief or remedy, or make such order, within its jurisdiction as it considers just and appropriate. This may include an award of damages. Damages will only be awarded by a court which has the power to make an award of damages or to order the payment of compensation in civil proceedings (s 8).

REMEDIES UNDER THE HUMAN RIGHTS ACT 1998

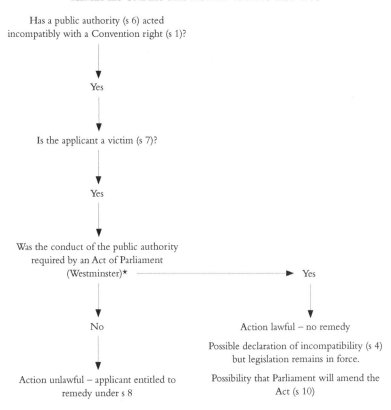

Has a public authority (s 6) acted
incompatibly with a Convention right (s 1)?

Yes

Is the applicant a victim (s 7)?

Yes

Was the conduct of the public authority
required by an Act of Parliament
(Westminster)★ ──────────────────────▶ Yes

No   Action lawful – no remedy

                                            Possible declaration of incompatibility (s 4)
                                            but legislation remains in force.

Action unlawful – applicant entitled to   Possibility that Parliament will amend the
remedy under s 8   Act (s 10)

The right to seek a remedy for infringement of Convention rights under
international law still exists. The United Kingdom granted the right of
individual petition to the European Court of Human Rights in 1966 and
has since renewed it every 5 years.

Frequently Asked Questions

*Is it necessary to have both the Human Rights Act 1998 and the Scotland Act
1998?*

The human rights protection afforded by the relevant sections of the
Scotland Act is very important as it gives a right to challenge not only acts

---

★ *Note*: the defence of statutory authority applies only to Acts of the UK Parliament. Acts
of the Scottish Parliament and provisions under secondary legislation may be declared
invalid.

of the Scottish Administration, but also Acts of the Scottish Parliament. Actions against public authorities in Scotland which are not part of the Scottish Administration are brought under the Human Rights Act.

Can the Human Rights Act 1998 be repealed?

The Human Rights Act 1998 is an ordinary Act of Parliament and can therefore be amended or repealed through ordinary parliamentary procedures.

Essential Facts

Scotland Act 1998

- An Act of the Scottish Parliament is not law in so far as any provision of the Act is outside the legislative competence of the Parliament (s 29(1)).
- A challenge to an Act of the Scottish Parliament can be initiated by law officers and ordinary citizens via the process of judicial review (s 101). A challenge to the competence of an Act can arise in another type of action, eg as part of one's defence on a statutory criminal charge.

Human Rights Act 1998

- A court or tribunal determining a question which has arisen in connection with a Convention right must take into account judgments, decisions, declarations or advisory opinions of the European Court of Human Rights (s 2(1)).
- Legislation must be interpreted in a manner which is compatible with Convention rights (s 3).
- If a judge is convinced that primary unambiguous legislation is inconsistent with the Convention, he can make a declaration of incompatibility (s 4).
- All public authorities must act in a way which complies with the European Convention on Human Rights (s 6).
- All UK legislation must have a "statement of compatibility" from the relevant Government Minister (s 19).
- All legislation, old and new, must be interpreted and given effect by judges, as far as possible and be Convention compliant (s 3).
- Courts must pay "particular regard" in relevant circumstances to the importance of freedom of expression, thought, conscience and religion (ss 12 and 13).

- A person may bring proceedings under the Human Rights Act if he is a victim and believes that there has been an infringement of his Convention rights by a public authority (s 7(1) and (6)).
- Private bodies and individuals are not required by the Human Rights Act to respect Convention rights.

Essential Cases

Klass v Germany (1979–80) and **Re S; Re W (2002)**: applicant must be a victim.

R v A (No 2) (2002): considers when judges should interpret statutes and when they should resort to a declaration of incompatibility.

A v Secretary of State for the Home Department (2004) (the *Belmarsh* case): detention of terrorist suspects. Declaration of incompatibility.

R (Daly) v Home Secretary (2003): the Human Rights Act does not require courts to review the merits of administrative decisions. Courts should apply the legal test of "proportionality".

3 FUNDAMENTAL RIGHTS

The fundamental rights are those which are absolute and subject to no possibility of derogation. They cannot be restricted and they are not balanced against any public interest arguments. They include the right to life (Art 2), the prohibition of torture and inhuman and degrading treatment (Art 3), the prohibition of slavery (Art 4) and the freedom from punishment without law (Art 7).

RIGHT TO LIFE

Article 2 provides:

> "1 Everyone's right to life shall be protected by law. No one shall be deprived of his life save in the execution of a sentence of a court following his conviction of a crime for which this penalty is provided by law.
>
> 2 Deprivation of life shall not be regarded as inflicted in contravention of this Article when it results from the use of force which is no more than absolutely necessary:
>
> (a) in defence of any person from unlawful violence;
>
> (b) in order to effect a lawful arrest or to prevent the escape of a person lawfully detained;
>
> (c) in action lawfully taken for the purpose of quelling a riot or insurrection."

The way in which the article is set out is typical of the articles relating to substantive rights. Paragraph (1) states the general right, ie that everyone's right to life is protected; and para (2) explains and qualifies this by setting out three sets of circumstances in which the deprivation of life is not unlawful provided that unnecessary force has not been used.

The most obvious effect of Art 2 is to provide protection against deliberate or negligent killing by state officials. It did not, however, prohibit the death penalty. Protection against the death penalty is now provided by Protocol 6, which has been ratified by the United Kingdom, and abolished the death penalty in peace time. More recently, Art 1 of Protocol 13 states that the death penalty shall be abolished in all circumstances. Article 2 is interpreted with regard to its fundamental importance in the Convention.

Its provisions must be strictly construed. The Article establishes a demanding test to ensure that any force deployed by the state must not have been in excess of what was absolutely necessary

Positive obligation

As well as providing protection against the arbitrary use of force by state officials, Art 2 may impose duties upon a state to take positive steps to preserve life. There have been many attempts to extend the meaning of Art 2 to encompass areas not perhaps envisaged by the original drafters.

Areas involving probable duty under Art 2 include the following:

- use of force by the state;
- death in custody;
- protection for individual against imminent threats of violence from others;
- responsibility to minimise the risk of harm from noxious and potentially lethal pollutants.

Areas involving possible duty under Art 2 include the following:

- denial of health care;
- withdrawal of medical treatment;
- deportation or extradition.

Areas involving no duty under Art 2 include the following:

- adequacy of social benefits to sustain life;
- prevention of abortion;
- assisted suicide.

Use of force

The second paragraph of Art 2 permits the use of force but only where it is strictly necessary. In the case of *McCann, Farrell and Savage* v *United Kingdom* (1995) the European Court of Human Rights ruled that the action of soldiers in shooting three Irish Republican Army members in Gibraltar was justified, in the light of the information available to the security forces at the time. The decisions taken by the authorities, however, amounted to unlawful action. The operation should have been more tightly controlled so that the suspected terrorists were not killed. In order to be lawful the action must be proportionate to the circumstances in each case. In the *McCann* case the European Court commented on the investigation into the deaths and the inquest proceedings and it has been held to be important that there is an effective investigation of any deaths or injuries caused by the use of force by state authorities.

In *Kelly* v *United Kingdom* (1993) soldiers shot dead a joyrider who sped through a military checkpoint. It was held that the use of force was justified in the circumstances and there was no violation of Art 2. In *Stewart* v *United Kingdom* (1984) a soldier was aiming a rubber bullet at the legs of a rioter when he was struck by a brick and his gun went off. The rubber bullet hit a young boy on the head and killed him. There was no question of a deliberate killing and the Commission found that, although Art 2 applied, the soldier's action was lawful under para 2 of the Article

Duty to safeguard life

The responsibility of the state under Art 1 also includes a duty to protect the lives of people living within the jurisdiction. This may amount to a positive obligation to take preventative measures to protect a person or persons who may be at risk because of the criminal acts of another. In *Osman* v *UK* (2000), a teacher became obsessed with a pupil and committed some minor offences against him and made death threats. The police were aware of the situation but took no measures to protect the boy or his family. The teacher murdered the boy's father and another person. The European Court of Human Rights held that the authorities had known that there was a real and immediate threat to life and should have taken steps to protect the boy and his family. The key principle of the judgment is that "... the first sentence of art 2(1) enjoins the state not only to refrain from intentional and unlawful taking of life but also to take appropriate steps to safeguard the lives of those within its jurisdiction".

There have been cases where it has been determined that the state may need to take positive steps to protect the life of an individual, for example by granting him anonymity, or even a new identity, even where the risk of reprisals might have arisen because of the wrongful act of the individual. The case of *R* v *Lord Saville of Newdigate, ex parte B (No 2)* (2000) concerned the proceedings of a tribunal set up to inquire into the circumstances of the "Bloody Sunday" shootings in 1972. A decision was taken to withdraw anonymity from individual soldiers who had admitted firing guns. It was held that it was not necessary to reveal the soldiers' identity in order to achieve the tribunal's purpose of determining the truth. The tribunal had neglected to give sufficient weight to the risk of reprisals against the soldiers. The individual right to life was a fundamental freedom to which the tribunal had possibly paid insufficient attention.

Another high-profile case was *Venables and Thompson* v *News Group Newspapers Ltd* (2001). Venables and Thompson had been convicted of the murder of 2-year-old James Bulger when they were 10 years old. When they were due to be released from custody they sought permanent injunctions to prevent the press disclosing their whereabouts or their adult appearance. They based their claim on Art 2 and Art 3. The Press relied on Art 10 and argued that injunctions would limit their freedom of expression. Permanent injunctions were granted as a failure to do so could have led to serious injury or death.

Death in custody

The state has an obligation to investigate the death of a person who has been held in the custody of the police or prison authorities. The investigation should be sufficiently rigorous and transparent so that an explanation can be given for the death and appropriate action taken. The lack of effective investigation may itself amount to a breach of Art 2, as was found in *Salman* v *Turkey* (2002). A person had died while he was in custody. When there is a death in custody there is a particularly stringent obligation on the authorities to provide a satisfactory and convincing explanation for the death. Where there is no satisfactory explanation the responsibility for the death would lie with the state.

In Scotland, the Procurator Fiscal is informed when a death in custody occurs. He or she will instigate an investigation, report his findings to the Lord Advocate and a fatal accident inquiry will be held under the Fatal Accidents and Sudden Deaths Inquiry (Scotland) Act 1976 (unless there is to be a trial in relation to the incident). A fatal accident inquiry is mandatory where a person has died while in police custody. At the end of the inquiry the sheriff will set out the details of the occurrence leading to the death, any reasonable precautions which might have prevented the death and any other relevant facts. He has no power to make findings of fault or to apportion blame for the incident. This means that, where the death has been caused by a breach of Art 2, further proceedings may be necessary to secure a remedy.

There is a requirement to safeguard a prisoner while he is in custody and this may extend to taking reasonable steps to prevent him from committing suicide. In *Keenan* v *United Kingdom* (2001), a mentally disturbed prisoner, who was being held in segregation in a punishment block, committed suicide. His mother sought a ruling that proper steps had not been taken to safeguard his life and that placing him in the punishment block amounted to inhuman and degrading treatment under Art 3. The Court held that there was a duty to safeguard life but it was unable to find that there had been a breach of duty in the particular case as the medical practitioners had disagreed about the diagnosis of the patient and the extent to which he was at risk of suicide.

Euthanasia and the withdrawal of medical treatment

Hospitals must consider the rights of the individual when they are making decisions about treating patients but this does not mean that every decision which leads to a loss of life will be unlawful. In *Widmar* v *Switzerland* (1993) the Commission declared that there was no requirement under Art 2 for states to make passive euthanasia a criminal offence. It would be a breach of the Convention for a state to sanction mercy killing. In other words, it is not always unlawful for life-saving treatment to be withdrawn but positive interventions which cause a person to die may be unlawful.

In September 2000, doctors in England had to make a harrowing choice: whether to separate conjoined ("Siamese") twins and allow one child to live but cause the other to die, or to leave them conjoined with the inevitable result that they would both die in a few months. The doctors wished to operate but the parents opposed the decision. In *Re A (Children) (Conjoined Twins: Medical Treatment) (No 1)* (2001) it was held that the operation to separate conjoined twins could go ahead even though the death of one child was the inevitable result of the procedure. The right of life for one child who had a good chance of having a reasonable quality of life outweighed the right of the other child who could not survive since she was dependent on her sister's vital organs.

In 1996, the Scottish Courts considered whether it would be in the best interests of a woman in a persistent vegetative state to discontinue the treatment of artificial feeding and hydration. In *Law Hospital NHS Trust* v *Lord Advocate* (1996), the Court of Session held that the court had power to authorise the discontinuation of life-sustaining treatment where the patient was permanently insensate and unconscious. After this case the Lord Advocate issued a statement clarifying the criminal law and confirming that no criminal prosecution would follow a decision to withdraw treatment provided that permission had been granted by a civil court.

This case followed the decisions in several English cases, including *Airedale NHS Trust* v *Bland* (1993), where a victim of the Hillsborough football stadium disaster was in a persistent vegetative state and his parents and the hospital sought permission to discontinue his treatment. The House of Lords had made it clear that their decision only applied to patients in a persistent vegetative state and that any decision to withdraw treatment in similar circumstances would need the approval of the High Court.

Abortion and rights of the foetus

There are arguments put forward to the effect that a state which legalises abortion is in contravention of Art 2. This question has been considered by the European Court of Human Rights or the Commission on a number of occasions. In *Paton* v *United Kingdom* (1980), the Commission held that there was no breach of Art 2 if an abortion was carried out at an early stage of pregnancy to protect the health of the mother. It was stated that:

> "the life of the foetus is intimately connected with, and cannot be regarded in isolation of, the pregnant woman. If article 2 were held to cover the foetus and its protection under the article was seen as absolute, an abortion would have to be considered as prohibited even where the continuance of the pregnancy would involve a serious risk to the life of the pregnant woman. This would mean that the unborn life of the foetus would be regarded as being of higher value than the life of the pregnant woman".

The judges of the European Court of Human Rights have avoided pronouncing on the rights of the foetus, perhaps because this is a subject on which there is no consensus among the states. Any case before the European Court of Human Rights requires that the applicant must be a victim. A foetus has the potential for life but is not experiencing life. Therefore a foetus has the potential to become a victim but will only do so after it has been born alive. The domestic law of the United Kingdom has consistently taken this approach and ruled that the legal protection of the person commences at birth. In Great Britain, abortion is regulated by the Abortion Act 1967, as amended by s 37 of the Human Fertilisation and Embryology Act 1990. The 1967 Act allows termination of pregnancy where the pregnancy has lasted less than 24 weeks and:

(a) its continuation would involve greater risk to the physical or mental health of the mother or any existing children; or

(b) there is grave risk of permanent injury or death to her; or

(c) there is a substantial risk that the child would suffer from serious disability.

The law concerning abortion is a reserved matter under the Scotland Act 1998, ie the power to legislate in relation to abortion is reserved to the Westminster Parliament.

A key Scottish case concerning the right of the foetus is that of *Kelly* v *Kelly* (1997). The estranged husband of a pregnant woman sought an interdict to prevent her having an abortion. The man argued that, as he was the biological father, he was the guardian of the unborn child and should have a right to petition the court on behalf of the unborn child. The Court of Session concluded that "Scots Law conferred no right on the foetus to continue to reside in its mother's womb". The abortion was not a civil wrong and the father had no right to prevent the abortion taking place.

Assisted suicide

The question whether the state has a duty to prevent suicide by imposing criminal penalties on those who provide assistance to someone committing suicide has been the subject of a number of recent cases in the United Kingdom. The Suicide Act 1961 abolished the crime of suicide in England and Wales but retained the crime of aiding and abetting, counselling or procuring the suicide of another, and thus it is an offence to assist someone to end their own life. Suicide is not a crime in Scotland but a person who attempts to commit suicide in a public place could be charged with breach of the peace. Someone who provides assistance could be charged with culpable homicide.

In late 2001, Diane Pretty, who suffered from motor neuron disease, sought judicial review of a decision that her husband might be prosecuted if he assisted her to die. Diane Pretty wished to take her own life but her physical incapacity meant that she required physical assistance from another to end her life. Her petition was refused by the House of Lords and she took her case to the European Court of Human Rights (*Pretty v United Kingdom* (2002)). She submitted that Art 2, when read in conjunction with Protocol 6, Art 1 and Protocol 6, Art 2 of the Convention guaranteed that an individual could choose whether or not to live. She alleged also that the refusal of the Director of Public Prosecutions to provide an undertaking that her husband would not be prosecuted for helping her to die submitted him to inhuman and degrading treatment in breach of Art 3. The European Court of Human Rights held that Art 2 could not be used in this way to guarantee the right to end life. Articles 2 and 3 were complementary to each other and there was nothing in Art 3 that affected an individual's right to choose not to live. Art 2 does not confer a right of self- determination in the sense of conferring on the individual the entitlement to choose death rather than life. The refusal of the United Kingdom authorities to give Mr Pretty immunity from prosecution did not constitute inhuman or degrading treatment; nor did the fact that she would face an undignified and distressing death amount to interference with her right to respect for private life under Art 8(1). As the purpose of the laws which prevent aiding and abetting suicide are intended to protect the weak and vulnerable, it was not disproportionate to make assisted suicide unlawful.

In the aftermath of this case there have been a number of other cases which have been decided on similar grounds. Bills proposing that assisted suicide should be made legal in certain circumstances have been laid before both the Westminster Parliament and the Scottish Parliament. Assisting someone to end their life is still a crime.

PROHIBITION OF TORTURE

Article 3 states:

> "No one shall be subject to torture or to inhuman or degrading treatment or punishment."

This article is written in uncompromising and unqualified terms. It protects people from three different types of treatment.

- Torture: involves intense physical suffering and a probability of actual bodily injury.
- Inhuman treatment: may involve mental or physical suffering of a lesser degree.
- Degrading treatment: is the sort of treatment which arouses feelings of fear, anguish and inferiority.

Although the interpretation of these terms is sometimes a matter of degree, it has been clearly established that they are not synonymous; however, the limits of each have not been fully settled.

Torture

"Torture" was defined in *Ireland* v *United Kingdom* (1979–80) as "deliberate inhuman treatment causing very serious and cruel suffering". The case concerned 14 people who had been interrogated by UK security forces in 1971. The security forces used a number of different interrogation techniques including sleep deprivation, deprivation of food and drink, hooding and subjecting to continuous loud noise. None of the internees were physically injured but some suffered psychiatric symptoms. The Court decided that the treatment of suspected terrorists did not reach the level of suffering of particular intensity and cruelty implied by the word "torture", but did constitute inhuman and degrading treatment. The level of severity will depend on all of the circumstances of the case and the Court will take into account such factors as the duration of the maltreatment, its physical and mental effect on the applicant and, where appropriate, the age, health and sex of the applicant.

Inhuman treatment or punishment.

The treatment which was suffered by the detainees in *Ireland* v *United Kingdom* (1979–80) was found to have caused physical and mental suffering but not to have been sufficiently cruel and intense as to amount to torture. This is an area where the fact that the European Convention on Human Rights is a devolving and living instrument is significant. The sort of treatment which was regarded as falling short of the standard of torture 40 years ago may be regarded as unacceptable now. In *Aydin* v *Turkey* (1998) the victim was a 17-year-old Kurdish girl who was suspected of being a Kurdish separatist or sympathiser. She was detained at a police station where she was blindfolded, beaten, stripped, placed inside a tyre, sprayed with a high-pressure hose and finally raped. This conduct would probably not have been regarded as reaching the threshold of severity to be regarded as torture but the Court held that the accumulation of acts of physical and mental violence constituted torture.

Degrading treatment

Treatment or punishment will be degrading if the victim has feelings of fear, anguish or inferiority. In *Tyrer* v *United Kingdom* (1979–80) a 15-year-old boy on the Isle of Man pleaded guilty to a charge of assault and was sentenced to be birched the same day. He had to wait for some hours until the police doctor arrived and then he was held down by two police officers and beaten with the birch. The European Court did not find that the action amounted to torture or inhuman treatment but did hold that it constituted degrading treatment. A key factor was that the victim had been made to undress.

The European Court of Human Rights has stated that the threat of inhuman or degrading treatment may itself be sufficient to breach Art 3. In the case of *Campbell and Cosans* v *United Kingdom* (1982) two mothers claimed that the use of the tawse (belt) in Scottish schools was a degrading punishment. The Court accepted that a sufficiently real and immediate threat of infliction of treatment could violate Art 3 but, as neither of the children in the case had been beaten with the tawse nor threatened with such punishment, the Court decided in favour of the parents on other grounds. In *Keenan* v *United Kingdom* (2001) a mentally disturbed prisoner, who was being held in segregation in a punishment block, committed suicide. It was held that the decision to place him in the punishment block for 7 days amounted to inhuman and degrading treatment under Art 3.

The most notable case relating to Art 3 after the Scotland Act 1998 and the Human Rights Act 1998 came into force is *Napier* v *Scottish*

Ministers (2004). A prisoner who was held on remand in Barlinnie Prison petitioned for judicial review, claiming that the conditions in which he was held amounted to inhuman and degrading treatment. It was held that to detain a person along with another prisoner in a cramped cell for 20 hours per day, with no sanitation facilities and no activity other than daily walking exercise for 1 hour and a weekly recreation period of 1½ hours was degrading treatment, infringing Art 3. He was awarded damages of £2,000.

Positive obligation

Article 3 clearly creates an obligation on a state to refrain from ill-treating people within its jurisdiction. It also may create a positive obligation on the state to protect individuals from torture and inhuman and degrading treatment by others. In *A* v *United Kingdom* (1998), a 9-year-old boy applied to the European Court of Human Rights, claiming that the state had failed to protect him from ill-treatment by his stepfather. He had been beaten regularly with a garden cane. The man had been prosecuted for assault causing actual bodily harm but had been acquitted after the jury accepted his defence that he had used reasonable force to chastise a difficult child. The Court held that, by failing to provide adequate legal protection, the state had not fulfilled its responsibility under Art 1 to secure to everyone within its jurisdiction the rights and freedoms of the Convention.

In *Z* v *United Kingdom* (2002) damages were awarded to children on the basis that the state had failed to protect them from serious neglect and ill-treatment by their parents over a period of 4½ years. Support had been given to the family by social services but no steps had been taken to place the children in care, despite police and social services reports which had identified significant abuse and neglect. It was held that there is a positive obligation on a state to take steps to prevent such treatment.

Note that if the Art 3 threshold for degrading treatment is not reached, a victim may still have a right to a remedy under Art 8, which also covers the integrity of the person.

PROHIBITION OF SLAVERY AND FORCED LABOUR

Article 4 states that;

> "1 No one shall be held in slavery or servitude.
>
> 2 No one shall be required to perform forced or compulsory labour.

3 For the purpose of this Article the term 'forced or compulsory labour' shall not include:

(a) any work required to be done in the ordinary course of detention imposed according to the provisions of Art 5 of this Convention or during conditional release from such detention;

(b) any service of military character or, in case of conscientious objectors in countries where they are recognised, service exacted instead of compulsory military service;

(c) any service exacted in case of emergency or calamity threatening the life or well-being of the community;

(d) any work or service which forms part of normal civic obligations."

Contraventions of this provision are unlikely to arise in modern democratic states and so there is little case law. The Article is most frequently invoked by individuals who complain about work that they are required to carry out while in detention, or services that the state required them to provide for others. Community service orders for offenders are deemed to be lawful under Art 4(3)(a) as an order is imposed only if the offender consents to it. (Criminal Procedure (Scotland) Act 1995, s 238(2)).

There has never been a successful claim under Art 4 although the application in *Schmidt* v *Germany* (1994) was partially successful on other grounds. Schmidt challenged the rule that German men were required to serve as firemen or pay a fire service levy instead. The same obligation was not placed upon women. He claimed that he was the victim of discrimination on the ground of sex contrary to the European Convention on Human Rights 1950, Art 14 in conjunction with Art 4(3)(d). It was held, that compulsory fire service was one of the normal civic obligations within Art 4(3)(d). The obligation to pay a contribution in lieu of service also came within Art 4(3)(d). There had, however, been a breach of Art 14 as the difference in treatment between men and women was discriminatory and unjustified.

FREEDOM FROM RETROACTIVE CRIMINAL CONVICTIONS OR PENALTIES

Article 7 states:

"1 No one shall be held guilty of an offence on account of any act or omission which did not constitute a criminal offence under national or international law at the time when it was committed.

Nor shall a heavier penalty be imposed than the one that was applicable at the time the criminal offence was committed.

2 This Article shall not prejudice the trial and punishment of any person for any act or omission which, at the time when it was committed, was criminal according to the general principles of law recognised by civilised nations."

Article 7 relates exclusively to criminal proceedings. The first paragraph deals with the broad principles of criminal law. The second paragraph allows the prosecution of people for crimes of an international nature such as war crimes, so that people cannot escape punishment because the crime was not specified in the domestic legislation at the time that it was committed, provided that, at the time it was committed, it was an affront to general international legal principles.

War crimes

The War Crimes Act 1991 allowed the prosecution of individuals for their alleged criminal actions during the Second World War. Prosecutions could be brought for crimes alleged to have been committed in Germany or in German Occupied territory. The Act could have been subject to challenge if Art 7(1) stood alone, but the type of crime involved came within the category of conduct provided for in the qualifying section, Art 7(2).

Article 7(1) contains two principles:

- a person can only be convicted of a crime which existed at the time it was allegedly committed,
- the penalty imposed should not be more severe than applied at the time of the offence.

The prohibition on the creation of retroactive criminal offences applies to offences created by legislation and by the development of the common law. However, the gradual clarification of the rules of criminal liability through judicial interpretation may be allowed provided that the development is consistent with a general trend in the development of the criminal law and is reasonably foreseeable.

New crimes

In *SW* v *United Kingdom* and *CR* v *United Kingdom* (1996) the applicants had been charged with the rape or attempted rape of their wives. At the time the offences were committed rape within marriage was regarded as an exemption to the general law of rape. It was clear that, over a period of years in a series of judicial decisions, the immunity of the husband from prosecution for rape no longer existed. The applicants claimed that their prosecutions violated Art 7 as rape within marriage was not a crime when they committed the acts. The European Court of Human Rights held that there was no violation of Art 7 because the case law had evolved in a consistent and foreseeable way. It was held in *Scottish Ministers* v *McGuffie* (2006) that the confiscation of property under Pt 5 of the Proceeds of Crime Act 2006 did not amount to a retrospective criminal penalty.

In Scotland, the High Court of Justiciary retains a declaratory power which allows it to declare the ambit of a known crime, or to criminalise an action which was formerly not known to be criminal. In practice it is only used in very limited circumstances. It has long been accepted that the power might be exercised in respect of an act or omission which is both in itself wrong and hurtful to the persons or property of another. The case of *Khaliq* v *HM Advocate* (1983) is a modern example of the use of the declaratory power by the High Court of Justiciary. A successful prosecution was brought against a shopkeeper who had sold "glue-sniffing kits" consisting of small amounts of glue in plastic bags to children. There was no specific legal prohibition of this conduct at the time but it was argued that the conduct was clearly wrong and harmful to the children. There is little doubt that the exercise of the declaratory power could be contrary to Art 7(1) unless very careful regard is given to the circumstances in which it is used.

Legal certainty

The law needs to be as precise and definite as possible so that a person can know, with a reasonable degree of certainty, whether his conduct may result in a criminal prosecution. In *Kokkinakis* v *Greece* (1994), the Court observed that the requirement that an offence be clearly defined by law "is satisfied where the individual can know from the wording of the relevant provision and, if need be, with the assistance of the court's interpretation of it, what acts and omissions will make him liable". There are two offences in Scots law which are particularly vague and therefore may not be Convention compliant.

Breach of the peace and shameless indecency

The offence of breach of the peace covers a wide range of circumstances and has been very broadly interpreted. Successful prosecutions have related to conduct such as peeping over a wall to watch women using a solarium and eating an ice cream in a suggestive manner in a public place. Breach of the peace requires proof of an actual disturbance or "... of something done in breach of public order or decorum which could reasonably be expected to lead to the lieges being alarmed or upset". (The term "lieges" simply means any member of the public.) Shameless indecency is another offence with a rather vague definition. Again there is a broad range of circumstances where this offence has been charged, including indecent assault by a man on other men and showing an obscene film to two teenage girls in private premises. If the circumstances surrounding a prosecution of either of these offences are within the boundaries previously established by the case law, then arguably the offences of breach of the peace and shameless indecency will not be incompatible with Art 7.

Increased penalties

The second sentence of Art 7(1) refers to a prohibition on heavier penalties being imposed than those which applied at the time an offence was committed. It is assumed in both Scots and English law that a statute increasing a penalty for an offence will not take effect retrospectively unless there is a clear and explicit statement that it does. In recent years, advances in forensic investigation of crime, such as DNA testing have led to a number of prosecutions for crimes committed some years ago. Prosecution authorities face a difficult task in ensuring that an accused person is prosecuted under the legislation pertaining at the time of the offence and that the penalty imposed does not exceed the range of available penalties at the time of the offence.

Frequently Asked Questions

Is it contrary to Art 1 for doctors to comply with "do not resuscitate notices"?

If it would be futile to revive someone and take active measures to keep them alive when they are suffering great pain and will die in the near future, cases on this matter have recognised that to keep someone alive in such circumstances may be breach of Art 3. The situation when someone has decided that they do not wish to be resuscitated in the event of losing consciousness is less clear. It is likely that there will be a clear statement of the legal situation in the near future.

Why has assisted suicide not been made legal in the UK?

Although there are many campaigners wishing to introduce laws to make it legal for a person to assist another to die, it is a very complex matter and any laws which are introduced will need to include strong safeguards so that there is no risk of abuse by people who wish to end the lives of their relatives for ulterior motives.

Should the crime of breach of the peace be replaced with a series of specific statutory offences?

It has been argued that this would make the law more certain and accessible as people would have a clearer knowledge of what amounts to an offence. The reality, though, is that this could make the law very complex and possibly more obscure. Breach of the peace has long been regarded as a useful way of dealing with a broad range of activities which undeniably should be suppressed. Providing that the decisions taken by judges are conservative and prosecutions only succeed only when the conduct is of the type which a reasonable person would expect to be contrary to the criminal law, then the current situation is reasonably fair and very effective.

Essential Facts

- Articles 2, 3, 4 and 7 are fundamental rights. They are absolute and subject to no possibility of derogation. They cannot be restricted and they are not balanced against any public interest arguments.
- Article 2 is concerned with the right to life.
- Article 2 imposes a duty on the state not to engage in unlawful killing. It also may create a positive obligation to protect persons within its jurisdiction from being killed unlawfully by others.
- Article 3 is concerned with the prohibition of torture and inhuman and degrading treatment.
- The distinction between torture and inhuman treatment is a question of the severity of the suffering, taking into account all of the circumstances.
- Degrading treatment is treatment which invokes feelings of fear, anxiety and inferiority.
- Article 4 is concerned with the prohibition of slavery. Few cases have been brought under Art 4 – it is more likely that issues such as people trafficking will be dealt with by other legal measures at national level.
- The declaratory power of the High Court of Justiciary could potentially be incompatible with Art 7.

Essential Cases

Re A (Children) (Conjoined Twins: Medical Treatment) (No 1) (2001): medical treatment certain to cause one death but save another – no breach of Art 2.

Law Hospital NHS Trust v Lord Advocate (1996): withdrawal of medical treatment – lawful in the case of persistent vegetative state.

McCann, Farrell and Savage v United Kingdom (1995): use of force by state must be no more than is reasonable in the circumstances.

Kelly v United Kingdom (1993): killing by state officials may be lawful if justified.

Osman v United Kingdom (2000): obligation on state to safeguard life.

Widmar v Switzerland (1993): passive euthanasia is not always unlawful.

Paton v United Kingdom (1980): Art 2 does not prohibit abortion.

Kelly v Kelly (1997): foetus does not have rights under Art 2.

Pretty v United Kingdom (2002): right to life does not include a right to die.

Venables and Thompson v News Group Newspapers Ltd (2001): James Bulger killers – duty on state to create new identities to protect their lives.

R v Lord Saville of Newdigate, ex parte B (No 2) (2000): Bloody Sunday inquiry – duty to preserve anonymity to prevent risk to life.

Ireland v United Kingdom (1979–80): definition of torture and inhuman treatment.

Campbell and Cosans v United Kingdom (1982): chance of corporal punishment by a school is not a breach of Art 3.

Z v United Kingdom (2002): obligation on state to safeguard children from inhuman and degrading treatment.

Napier v Scottish Ministers (2004): prison conditions may amount to inhuman and degrading treatment.

Schmidt v Germany (1994): ordinary civic obligations do not constitute slavery.

SW v United Kingdom and CR v United Kingdom (1996): no violation of Art 7 if criminal law develops consistently (rape within marriage).

Khaliq v HM Advocate (1983): declaratory power of the High Court of Justiciary (glue-sniffing kits).

4 PROCEDURAL RIGHTS

Procedural rights differ from the fundamental rights as it is possible for a state to derogate from the provisions of procedural rights. However, the state is not given the same amount of discretion to limit the rights as is afforded by the qualified rights. They are referred to as derogable, unqualified rights. The key procedural rights are the right to liberty (Art 5) and the right to a fair hearing (Art 6). Procedural rights can be limited only under explicit and finite circumstances defined in the Article itself.

RIGHT TO LIBERTY AND SECURITY

Article 5 states:

"1 Everyone has the right to liberty and security of person. No one shall be deprived of his liberty save in the following cases and in accordance with a procedure prescribed by law:

(a) the lawful detention of a person after conviction by a competent court;

(b) the lawful arrest or detention of a person for non-compliance with the lawful order of a court or in order to secure the fulfilment of any obligation prescribed by law;

(c) the lawful arrest or detention of a person effected for the purpose of bringing him before the competent legal authority on reasonable suspicion of having committed an offence or when it is reasonably considered necessary to prevent his committing an offence or fleeing after having done so;

(d) the detention of a minor by lawful order for the purpose of educational supervision or his lawful detention for the purpose of bringing him before the competent legal authority;

(e) the lawful detention of persons for the prevention of the spreading of infectious diseases, of persons of unsound mind, alcoholics, drug addicts or vagrants;

(f) the lawful arrest or detention of a person to prevent his effecting an unauthorised entry into the country or of a person against whom action is being taken with a view to deportation or extradition.

2 Everyone who is arrested shall be informed promptly, in a language which he understands, of the reasons for his arrest and of any charge against him.

3 Everyone arrested or detained in accordance with the provisions of paragraph 1(c) of this article shall be brought promptly before a judge or other officer authorised by law to exercise judicial power and shall be entitled to trial within a reasonable time or to release pending trial. Release may be conditioned by guarantees to appear for trial.

4 Everyone who is deprived of his liberty by arrest or detention shall be entitled to take proceedings by which the lawfulness of his detention shall be decided speedily by a court and his release ordered if the detention is not lawful.

5 Everyone who has been the victim of arrest or detention in contravention of the provisions of this Article shall have an enforceable right to compensation."

Introduction

Article 5 is one of the more important Articles within the Convention. As it is a procedural right, the circumstances in which a person may be deprived of his liberty are limited to the 15 grounds set out in the six sub-paragraphs of the Article. These include, for example, an individual awaiting deportation as an illegal immigrant, a convicted felon, an individual suspected of a criminal offence, someone awaiting lawful extradition, or detention for the person's well-being, or for the well-being of others (due to public health grounds), or in times of national emergency. Denial of a right to liberty under Art 5 may lead to further breaches of the Convention, eg the individual may be subjected to inhuman or degrading treatment, or deprived of a right to vote. The jurisprudence of the Convention reminds the judiciary that it must be mindful that any deprivation of liberty must be lawful and no longer than necessary in the circumstances.

The underlying aim of Art 5 is to ensure that no one should be deprived of their liberty in an arbitrary fashion. In *Kurt* v *Turkey* (1998) the European Court of Human Rights held:

"... the authors of the Convention reinforced the individual's protection against arbitrary deprivation of liberty imposed by Art 5 by guaranteeing a corpus of substantive rights which are intended to minimise the risks of arbitrariness by; allowing the act of deprivation of liberty to be amenable to independent judicial scrutiny and securing the accountability of the authorities for that act ...".

It must be noted that, prior to the implementation of the Scotland Act 1998 and the Human Rights Act 1998, some aspects of criminal procedure in Scots law could have been subject to challenge under the Convention. The Scottish Government introduced legislation in early 2000 to pre-empt legal challenges with regard to the provisions of the European Convention on Human Rights, especially concerning Art 5. These measures are found in the Bail, Judicial Appointments etc (Scotland) Act 2000 and the Convention Rights (Compliance) (Scotland) Act 2001.

Persons protected by Art 5

Article 5 provides that everyone has the right to liberty and security of person. "Everyone" means everyone within and subject to the jurisdiction and authority of the state concerned at home and abroad. Hence, the Convention applies to citizens and non-citizens of the state alike. Everyone shall be entitled to trial within a reasonable time and everyone shall be entitled to take proceedings by which the lawfulness of his detention shall be decided speedily by a court and his release ordered if the detention is not lawful.

Deprivation of liberty.

It is important to define a deprivation of liberty. A lack of liberty may not always involve physical detention and may not always have been achieved by force. The Court will pay particular regard to claims of breaches under Art 5, of the time, any force used and the nature of the confinement. In *De Wilde, Ooms and Versup v Belgium* (1971) the Court held that the fact that the defendant voluntarily handed himself into a police station was of no consequence to his rights of breach under Art 5. It was held that the right to liberty: "is too important in a democratic society within the meaning of the Convention for a person to lose the benefit of the protection of the Convention for the single reason that he gives himself up to be taken into detention. The detention might violate Art 5 even though the person concerned might have agreed to it". A similar decision was reached in *Ashingdane v United Kingdom* (1985) where the Court noted that Art 5 concerns the deprivation of liberty, rather than the place of the lawful detention.

The terms "arrest" and "detention" are used interchangeably in the text of Art 5. Hence, any arrest and detention must be interpreted as any measure, by national law (common or statute), to deprive an individual of his liberty. This can be a fine distinction, as was established in *Engel v The Netherlands* (1979–80), when confining military personnel to barracks was not a deprivation of liberty, but, locking them up in a gaol or guardroom in the barracks would be. In *Litwa v Poland* (2001) it was held that deprivation of liberty is only justified where "... other less severe measures, have been considered and found to be insufficient to safeguard the individual or public interest which might require that the person concerned be detained".

Legality of detention

The lawfulness of detention is an important concept which relates to both substance and procedure. Deprivation of liberty must not be arbitrary and must be fully in accordance with the state's national law and that of the Convention. It follows, therefore, that if the detention is unlawful under Scots law, it will also be in breach of Art 5. In *Kurt v Turkey* (1998) it was held "any deprivation of liberty must not only have been effected in conformity with the substantive and procedural rules of national law but must equally be in keeping with the very purpose of Art 5, namely to protect the individual from arbitrariness".

The "lawfulness" test requires that the detention is:

- prescribed by law;
- not in bad faith;
- not an abuse of authority; and
- fully compliant with substantive legal rules.

In *R (Wardle) v Leeds Crown Court* (2001) Lord Hope noted: "continued detention can be justified in a given case only if there are specific indications of a genuine requirement of public interest which, notwithstanding the presumption of innocence, outweighs the rule of respect for individual liberty".

Acts by private individuals

Much of Art 5 concerns actions by public authorities but there is also an obligation on the state to protect against an unlawful deprivation of liberty effected by others (*Storck v Germany* (2005)). Any non-public organisation or person charged with the responsibility of arresting an individual must ensure that the person, once arrested, is brought into the due legal processes immediately, in the same way as an individual arrested by a public official. In *Blume v Spain* (2000), the European Court of Human Rights held that

Spain was in violation of Art 5(1). A court order had been issued releasing members of a suspected cult to their families. The families then detained their relatives in a hotel in order that they could be deprogrammed by a mental health professional. It was held that the state had failed to protect their rights under Art 5.

Detention after conviction (Art 5(1)(a))

What constitutes a conviction?

A conviction is deemed to be the finding of guilt by a competent court, prescribed by law and adhering to the due processes of law. It may mean a court without a jury (such as a Court Martial) or another form of court. It also covers a person found guilty of committing an offence and detained in a mental health institution for treatment.

What constitutes a competent court?

This was considered in *De Wilde, Ooms and Versup* v *Belgium* (1971) where the Court concluded the Belgian Police court that ordered detention of an individual was not a court by the definition of the European Convention on Human rights. A police court, or decisions by a public prosecutor or military commander, do not fall within the definition of "a competent court" as required by the Convention. A court must:

- be independent of the executive and of the parties to the case;
- provide guarantees of judicial procedure.

Court orders and obligations prescribed by law (Art 5 (1)(b))

Detention may be a consequence of a failure to attend court, contempt of court, failure to pay a fine, or any other obligation by the court, such as residence restrictions etc. Deprivation of liberty to fulfil a contractual obligation is not permitted. In ascertaining the obligation prescribed by law, the European Court of Human Rights will look at the nature of the obligation and its subsequent effect. In *Lawless* v *Ireland* (1979–80), the Court held that there had to be a specific and concrete obligation. Once that obligation was identified, the person could be detained to fulfil the obligation.

Arrest or detention on suspicion of having committed an offence (Art 5(1)(c))

Under this Article it is permissible to arrest or detain a person in order to bring them before a competent court because one of three factors is present:

- reasonable suspicion that the person has committed an offence;
- detention is necessary to prevent the commission of an offence;
- detention is necessary to prevent the person fleeing after committing an offence.

An individual questioned by the police, detained and not charged with a criminal offence does not have grounds for a complaint about his deprivation of liberty under Art 5 unless there were no reasonable grounds for suspecting him of committing an offence. The European Court of Human Rights held in *Murray* v *United Kingdom* (1994) that, provided that the suspicion for detention is genuine, and the police officers concerned had reasonable suspicion, the detention will be lawful: "... facts which raise a suspicion need not be of the same level as those necessary to justify a conviction or even the bringing of a charge, which comes at the next stage of the process of criminal investigation". In *Dryburgh* v *Galt* (1981) Lord Wheatley noted that it did not matter whether the information on which a suspicion arises turns out to be ill-founded. It is the circumstances known to the police office at the time of the detention that are relevant, not the facts as subsequently ascertained.

The detention of minors (Art 5(1)(d))

Article 5(1)(d) involves two aspects, to detain a minor for educational purposes and to bring a minor before a competent legal authority. Detention for educational purposes must be genuinely concerned with education and not punitive incarceration. In *Boumar* v *Belgium* (1988) the Court held that it was lawful to hold a minor in an institution prior to placement in a reformatory facility but that holding a 16-year-old for a period of 199 days within a 1-year period, in a facility with no educational provision, was excessive and was a breach of the Convention. The European Court of Human Rights held in *Nielsen* v *Denmark* (1988) that the detention in a psychiatric hospital of a child against his will, though at the request of his mother, was not a deprivation of the minor's liberty but a responsible exercise by his mother of her custodial rights in the interests of the child.

Public health, mental illness and vagrancy (Art 5(i)(e))

Article 5(1)(e) covers five groups of people:

- those confined to prevent the spread of infectious disease;
- mentally ill people;
- alcoholics;
- drug addicts;
- vagrants.

Detention of persons for the prevention of the spreading of infectious diseases may be justified in an emergency situation such as a foot and mouth crisis or a health scare such as an influenza outbreak. The control of infectious diseases in Scotland is controlled by the Public Health (Scotland) Act 1897 as amended by the various National Health Service (Scotland) Acts.

In *Winterwerp* v *Netherlands* (1979), the Court established three criteria for the lawful detention of a person of unsound mind:

1 Even if an individual of unsound mind consented to such a deprivation of liberty, this would have to be subject to judicial decision.

2 The mental disorder(s) in question must be recognised by impartial medical expertise.

3 The degree of the mental disorder must be extreme.

In *Anderson* v *Scottish Ministers* (2002), the Privy Council considered Art 5(1)(e) when a challenge to the validity of the first Act passed by the Scottish Parliament (the Mental Health, Public Safety and Appeals (Scotland) Act 1999) was made. The Act, with retrospective effect, allowed the Scottish Ministers to detain individuals of a severe psychopathic personality disorders in a mental hospital to protect the public from harm. The Privy Council did not analyse the narrow focus of Art 5 but found that the Mental Health, Public Safety and Appeals (Scotland) Act was not incompatible with the Convention as the detention of the individuals was a proportionate means of protecting the public from harm.

The power to detain alcoholics under Art 5(1)(e) was considered in *Litwa* v *Poland* (2001). Mr Litwa was alleged to be drunk and verbally abusing post office staff. The police, it was held, deprived him of his liberty by placing him, unnecessarily, in a centre for alcoholics. The Court held that "... persons who are not medically diagnosed as 'alcoholics', but whose conduct and behavior under the influence of alcohol pose a threat to public order or themselves, can be taken into custody for the protection of the public or their own interests, such as their health or personal safety". Vagrants were defined in *De Wilde, Ooms and Versup* v *Belgium* (1971) as "persons who have no fixed abode, no means of subsistence and no regular trade or profession".

Immigration and extradition (Art 5(1)(f))

The European Court of Human Rights recognises that a state has a right of control over the residence, entry and deportation of aliens. As established in *Chahal* v *United Kingdom* (1997), Art 5(1)(f) allows for the lawful arrest and detention of those individuals the state believes is in breach of its immigration policies.

The arrest and detention is lawful only in the following circumstances:

- prevention of entry to the state concerned;
- for the purposes of deportation;
- the holding of a person awaiting extradition proceedings.

The arrest or detention of the individual concerned must be lawful and must not be arbitrary. When considering the period of detention permitted, the European Court of Human Rights requires requisite diligence. In *Lynas* v *Switzerland* (1976), the Commission stated: "if the proceedings are not conducted with requisite diligence or if the detention results from some misuse of authority it ceases to be justifiable under 5(1)(f). Within these limits the Commission might therefore have cause to consider the length of time spent in detention pending extradition". Three years' detention was regarded as justified in *Kolampar* v *Belgium* (1992).

Minimum rights for persons detained

The rest of Art 5 is concerned with stating the minimum rights for persons who are detained. They fall under three headings:

- reasons for detention (Art 5(2));
- trial within a reasonable time or release pending trial (Art 5(3));
- judicial determination of the lawfulness of the detention (Art 5(4)).

Article 5(5) then provides for compensation to be paid in the event of unlawful detention.

Reasons for detention

Everyone who is arrested shall be informed promptly, in a language which he understands, of the reasons for his arrest and of any charge against him. The use of the word "everyone" in Art 5(2) makes it clear that this right applies to all of the people within the jurisdiction of the state, and not just to citizens or residents. That the explanation must be in a language that the person understands allows the person concerned to know what is happening to him with a view to challenging the situation. In *Fox, Campbell and Hartley* v *United Kingdom* (1990), the Court held that an individual suspected by the police of a criminal offence must be told the "essential legal and factual grounds for his arrest", in order to allow the individual concerned to be able to challenge the legality of the detention before a court.

Within the text of the Article, "promptly" is used rather than "immediately". The time between being detained and being given an adequate justification for the suspicion will be balanced on a case-by-case basis. The Court has accepted intervals of between 2 hours (*Murray* v *United Kingdom* (1995)), and 19 hours (*Dikme* v *Turkey* (2000)). In deciding the interval period: the Court considers various factors affecting such a time period: for example, circumstances such as the finding of an interpreter, and the locus of the detention. In *Van der Leer* v *Netherlands* (1990) a 10-day interval before informing someone why they were confined to a mental institution was held by the Court to be unacceptable.

The "language which he understands" aspect of the Article has become a more significant responsibility with the growth of migration to states of the Convention. The language may have to be by signing or in braille; it also must be in non-technical, normal terms. If the person being detained has a low intellectual capability, then the authority detaining must seek professional advice on this matter to redress this imbalance.

Trial within a reasonable time or release pending trial (Art 5(3))

Under Scots law there are clearly defined procedural rules to ensure that cases are brought before the courts within a reasonable time. The periods vary according to the severity of the crime and whether or not the accused is being held in custody. The High Court of Justiciary, in *McDonald* v *PF, Elgin* (2003) held that a bail order of residence at home of 22 hours a day was not such a restriction as to amount to a deprivation of liberty under Art 5. The decision is probably inconsistent with Convention case law. The provisions of Art 5(3) lie at the heart of the due processes of criminal process protection. The Article requires two main issues to be addressed:

- prompt appearance before a judicial authority;
- trial within a reasonable time or release pending trial.

If an accused person is to be kept in custody, Art 5(3) requires that there be relevant and sufficient grounds for doing so. The grounds for the detention have to be tested in court and upheld by a judge or other authorised person. In *CC* v *United Kingdom* (1999) the Commission stated that the "judge must examine all the facts arguing for and against the existence of a genuine requirement of public interest justifying, with due regard to the presumption of innocence, a departure from the rule of respect for the accused's liberty".

In *Brogan* v *United Kingdom* (1989) the applicants were suspected IRA terrorists who were held for 4 days and 6 hours without charge. This was held to be too long. The United Kingdom subsequently indicated a derogation from Art 5(3) for situations where a public emergency occurs.

Judicial determination of the lawfulness of the detention (Art 5(4))

This part of the article allows the person in custody to challenge the lawfulness of his detention as speedily as possible. The challenge must relate to the legality of the detention itself and not its appropriateness. The European Court of Human Rights held in *Weeks* v *United Kingdom* (1988) that the role of the Home Secretary in England and Wales in deciding the release of a life prisoner was in breach of Art 5(4). The procedures have been altered to separate the security and punitive aspects of life sentences with impartial judicial control. In *Chahal* v *United Kingdom* (1997), the Court found a breach of Art 5(4), concerning the UK's immigration laws and the lack of provision, at the time, for challenge under judicial review, on grounds of national security. The length of time for the deportation period (5 years) was excessive.

In Scots law, measures have been put in place to ensure that the defence, during committal proceedings, is not in a disadvantaged position and the principle of equality of arms is upheld. The Crown provides a custody statement to the accused which details the evidence on which the case is based. The accused may then challenge the sufficiency of the evidence at the committal stage, although any challenge to the reliability of the evidence is a matter for the trial itself.

Compensation for unlawful detention (Art 5(5))

Where a judicial act is not in good faith – for example, if a decision to detain someone was made out of malice – s 8 of the Human Rights Act 1998 applies and damages should be awarded as appropriate. Where a judicial act is done in good faith, the Human Rights Act 1998, s 9(3) makes provision for the award of damages but only where the arrest or detention is in contravention of Art 5. In *Thompson* v *Commissioner of Police for the Metropolis* (1998) the Court of Appeal defined a guide for damages, an initial £500 per hour, and decreasing thereafter, to include if necessary aggravated damages, though not exceeding £50,000.

Derogations from Art 5

In 1998, following the *Brogan* case, a derogation from Art 5 was made under authority of the Prevention of Terrorism (Temporary Provisions) Act 1984 allowing for the detention of suspected terrorists for up to 7 days. It was confirmed by the Human Rights Act 1998, s 14(1)(a) for a period of 5 years but the peace settlement in Northern Ireland changed the emergency situation and the Terrorism Act 2000 provided for judicial authorisation of the detention of terrorist suspects. As a result of the Terrorism Act 2000, the derogation was no longer needed and the Government withdrew it in 2001. Shortly thereafter, due to the heightened threat of global terrorism, the United Kingdom entered a further derogation in relation to the detention of suspected international terrorists under the Anti-terrorism, Crime and Security Act 2001. In *A v Secretary of State for the Home Department* (2004) the House of Lords ruled that the measures for indefinite detention in the Act did not satisfy the conditions for derogating under Art 15 as the measures were not strictly required by the exigencies of the situation. The result was that the 2001 designated derogation order was quashed and a declaration of incompatibility was made in relation to s 23 of the Anti-terrorism, Crime and Security Act 2001 as being incompatible with Arts 5 and 14. The Prevention of Terrorism Act 2005 was consequently enacted to create a judicial structure under which the activities of suspected terrorists could be restricted and controlled. Section 1 of the Act gives the Secretary of State or the courts the powers to impose control orders for the purpose of protecting the public from terrorism.

Control orders

There are two types of control orders under the Prevention of Terrorism Act 2005:

- derogating orders – these are provisions which would constitute a breach of Art 5 and which are subject to a derogation from Art 5;
- non-derogating orders – these are provisions deemed to be compatible with Art 5.

Derogating orders	Non-derogating orders
Incompatible with Art 5 but covered by a derogation made by the Secretary of State	Compatible with Art 5

Derogating orders	Non-derogating orders
Must be made by a court on the application of the Secretary of State	May be made by the Secretary of State with the court's permission. In an emergency, may be made before the court gives permission
Function of the court: To make an order if: • on the balance of probabilities, the person has been involved in terrorism • the order is necessary to protect the public from a risk of terrorism • the risk arises out of a public emergency and there is a derogation from Art 5 in place • the obligations imposed by the control order are specified in the designation order.	Function of the court: To consider at an initial hearing the validity of the Secretary of State's decision to make an order At a full hearing, to assess whether there were grounds to issue the order
Power of the court: • to quash the order • to modify the obligations in the order	Power of the court: • to quash the order • to direct the Secretary of State to modify the order

Section 5 of the Prevention of Terrorism Act 2005 gives a power of arrest and detention for 48 hours where an application for a control order has been made and a constable considers that the person's arrest is necessary to ensure that he is given notice of the order when it is made.

The case of *Secretary of State for the Home Department* v *JJ* (2007) concerned a question as to whether non-derogating control orders contravened Art 5. Control orders with a large number of restrictions had been imposed on six foreign nationals. The Government argued that they did not contravene Art 5, and, if the measures were excessive, the correct action would be to direct an amendment of the control order, not to quash it. It was held that the Secretary of State had not had authority to make the order at the time he made it and so the whole order was invalid.

Right to a fair trial

Article 6 states:

"1 In the determination of his civil rights and obligations and of any criminal charge against him, everyone is entitled to a fair and public hearing within a reasonable time by an independent and impartial tribunal established by law. Judgment shall be pronounced publicly but the press and public may be excluded from all or part of the trial in the interests of morals, public order or national security in a democratic society, where the interests of juveniles or the protection of the private life of the parties so require, or to the extent strictly necessary in the opinion of the court in special circumstances where publicity would prejudice the interests of justice.

2   Everyone charged with a criminal offence shall be presumed innocent until proved guilty according to law.

3   Everyone charged with a criminal offence has the following minimum rights:

   (a) to be informed promptly, in a language which he understands and in detail, of the nature and cause of the accusation against him;

   (b) to have adequate time and facilities for the preparation of his defence;

   (c) to defend himself in person or through legal assistance of his own choosing or, if he has not sufficient means to pay for legal assistance, to be given it free when the interests of justice so require;

   (d) to examine or have examined witnesses against him and to obtain the attendance and examination of witnesses on his behalf under the same conditions as witnesses against him;

   (e) to have the free assistance of an interpreter if he cannot understand or speak the language used in court."

There have been more applications to the European Court of Human Rights concerning Art 6 than any other Article in the Convention. Article 6(1) concerns a general right in relation to both civil rights and obligations and criminal charges. Article 6(2) and (3) are concerned with the rights of persons charged with criminal offences.

   Article 6(1) is complex and contains several different elements. The sphere of its application is "civil rights and obligations" and "criminal charges". These terms are not necessarily given the same meanings by the European Court of Human Rights as those given by the Scottish courts. The right to a hearing within a reasonable time is a right which applies to civil as well as criminal proceedings and does not depend on a person being in custody. The right to a hearing before an independent and impartial tribunal is a right which has been raised as a devolution issue in several cases following the implementation of the Scotland Act 1998. The right to a fair hearing involves concepts such as the right to be heard and the right to know reasons, as well as a general right to fair treatment.

Meaning of "civil rights and obligations"

It is sometimes difficult to decide whether a case concerns what the European Court of Human Rights would regard as a civil right and obligation. The meaning of civil rights and obligations does not depend on the legal classification in domestic law but is an example of autonomous meaning for a Convention term encompassing rights and obligations of a civil character. Judicial processes will fall easily within the definition of "determining civil rights and obligations" but it is not always easy to determine which aspects of administrative decision-making fall within this category.

There are four elements which must be present for an issue to be regarded as involving a civil right or obligation:

- there must be a genuine claim or dispute;
- the dispute must relate to a right or obligation in domestic law;
- the right or obligation must be broadly civil in character;
- the outcome of the dispute must be directly decisive for the right or obligation.

Examples of civil rights and obligations have been held to include the following:

- *the right to claim compensation in relation to property*: in *Lithgow* v *United Kingdom* (1986) the Court held that the shareholders in shipbuilding companies nationalised by the Aircraft and Shipbuilding Industries Act 1977 were entitled to rely on Art 6(1);
- *planning determinations*: in *Lafarge Redland Aggregates Ltd* v *Scottish Ministers* (2001), Redland Aggregates, claimed that the Scottish Ministers were in breach of Art 6 in relation to the consideration of planning permission for the development of a "superquarry" on the Isle of Harris. It was held that Art 6 was applicable as property rights were clearly a civil right within the meaning of Art 6(1), and a breach of Art 6(1) had occurred in respect of the procedures followed.

Public authority	Examples of civil rights and obligations	Examples of rights and obligations which are not civil rights and obligations
Local government	Planning decisions Licensing decisions Public housing allocations Allocation of school places Access by parents of children taken into care Liability for negligence	Employment of staff Contracts with suppliers
University	Disciplinary procedures Appeal procedures	Academic decisions Employment of staff Contracts with students/ suppliers
Professional bodies, eg the Law Society	Disciplinary decisions Procedures for resolving disputes about membership	Assessment of qualifications
Central government	Social welfare benefits Immigration and deportation	Tax assessment Employment disputes with office holders such as police and armed forces

Meaning of "criminal charge"

If a national court classifies an act as a criminal offence, the European Court of Human Rights will not challenge this determination. There may be uncertainty, however, in relation to activities which are not classed as crimes. The Court regards the fact that an act is not classed as a crime or offence under national law as a relevant factor but not a definitive test. In the case of *Engel* v *Netherlands* (1976) the Court decided that even the fact that a person may be imprisoned as a punishment is not enough to categorise a matter as a criminal offence. Engel had committed offences against military discipline and had been punished by 2 days' arrest. In *McFeeley* v *United Kingdom* (1981), the Commission decided that a disciplinary hearing within a prison was not a determination of a criminal charge even though the consequences could include extended loss of liberty. This decision has been followed more recently in *Matthewson* v *Scottish Ministers* (2001). In *McIntosh* v *Lord Advocate* (2003), the Privy Council concluded that confiscation proceedings under s 3(2) of the Proceeds of

Crime (Scotland) Act 1995 would not be regarded as a criminal charge. Confiscation proceedings take place after a criminal conviction but the nature of the issue is one of civil rights and obligations.

Independent and impartial tribunals

Prior to 1998 the Scots law on fairness was based on the "twin pillars" of natural justice, ie absence of bias in the mind of the judge and a right to be heard. The requirement for a tribunal to be independent is a new dimension of the right to a fair hearing.

Principles for fairness prior to the Scotland Act 1998	Principles of fairness after 1998
Rule against bias – *Nemo judex in causa sua* (no one should be a judge in their own cause)	Rule against bias – *Nemo judex in causa sua*
Right to a hearing – *Audi alteram partem* (both sides have a right to be heard)	Right to a hearing
	Right to a hearing before an independent tribunal

In order for a court or tribunal to be independent and impartial in terms of Art 6(1), there are several conditions which must be met.

- security of tenure of the members;
- absence of bias among the members of the tribunal;
- absence of procedural unfairness.

Security of tenure of the tribunal members

In deciding whether a tribunal can be said to be independent, regard must be had to the following matters:

- the manner of appointment of its members;
- their term of office;
- the existence of guarantees against outside pressures;
- whether the body presents an appearance of impartiality.

They must not be subject to removal or reappointment at the whim of the Government.

Judicial appointments

In *Starrs* v *Ruxton* (2000), in the course of a criminal prosecution in Linthligow, it was argued that the sheriff court was not sufficiently independent to satisfy Art 6, when it was presided over by a temporary sheriff. Temporary sheriffs were appointed by the Secretary of State on the advice of the Lord Advocate, who also played a key role in the appointment of permanent sheriffs. It was argued that there may be a risk of an appearance of bias as a temporary sheriff may be unwilling to displease the Lord Advocate as he is also the head of the system of prosecution. Appointment as a temporary sheriff was widely regarded as a step towards appointment as a permanent sheriff. Possible hopes of such advancement, as well as the short-term nature of the office, compromised the independence of the temporary sheriff, and the High Court of Justiciary held that there was a breach of Art 6(1).

In *Clancy* v *Caird (No 1)* (2000), the situation was held to be different in the case of temporary judges. One of the parties to an action of damages before a temporary judge claimed that a temporary judge was not an independent and impartial tribunal. It was held that the appointment and use of temporary judges to hear cases did not breach Art 6 as temporary judges have security of tenure and enjoy the same status and immunities as a permanent judge.

Partly as a result of these two cases, the procedures for judicial appointment were reformed by the Bail, Judicial Appointments etc (Scotland) Act 2000. An independent Judicial Appointments Board was established; the use of temporary sheriffs has now been abolished.

The status of the district court came under consideration in the case of *Clark* v *Kelly* (2001). Kelly alleged that Kirkcaldy district court was not an independent and impartial tribunal under Art 6(1). The district court is presided over by a justice of the peace who has no legal qualifications and who determines both questions of fact and law. He or she is advised by a clerk of the district court, an official who is appointed and employed by the local authority. The clerk takes no part in deliberations on conviction or sentence. All fines imposed in a district court go to the local authority. The justices referred the matter to the High Court of Justiciary under the Scotland Act 1998, s 98 and Sch 6. It was held that, as the clerk of the district court does not act in a judicial capacity, there was no conflict with Art 6(1).

In order to ensure that some of the other bodies which exercise functions in relation to civic rights and obligations are sufficiently independent some further reforms were made by the Convention Rights (Compliance) (Scotland) Act 2001. The changes related to the procedures of the Parole Board for Scotland, the Court of the Lord Lyon (which deals with the law of arms and heraldry) and the Legal Aid Board.

Impartiality

Impartiality has two aspects:

- subjective freedom from bias or personal prejudice;
- impartiality from an objective viewpoint.

Prior to the implementation of the Scotland Act 1998 and the Human Rights Act 1998 the existing Scots law already had a well-established and clear set of principles of natural justice. The superior courts in their supervisory role over tribunals and administrative agencies require natural justice to be observed by many bodies which are not courts but which exercise powers and make decisions that directly affect the rights and interests of individuals. Breach of a rule of natural justice in which a body is required to act judicially will lead to its decisions being declared *ultra vires*.

Justice must be seen to be done

The two main principles of natural justice are: *audi alteram partem* (hear the other side), known as the right to a hearing, and *nemo judex in causa sua (potest)* (no one can be a judge in his own cause), known as the rule against bias. Underlying these there is a third principle that justice must not only be done but must manifestly be seen to be done. This is an objective test for bias which does not require any proof of actual bias in the mind of the decision-maker. In *Bradford* v *McLeod* (1986), during a national strike by coal miners, a sheriff made remarks at a social function to the effect that he "would not grant legal aid to miners". Subsequently, a miner represented by a solicitor who had heard these remarks appeared before that same sheriff, accused of breach of the peace on a picket line. The solicitor moved that the sheriff should declare himself disqualified from hearing the case because of the views that he had expressed. The sheriff declined to disqualify himself. The miner was convicted of the offence, as were 13 others in similar circumstances. They all sought to have their convictions and sentences suspended. It was held that there had been a miscarriage of justice. Although the sheriff himself might have been satisfied that he was not biased, circumstances existed which could create in the mind of a reasonable man a suspicion of the impartiality of the sheriff. It was not enough that justice was done; it must also be seen to be done.

The case of *Hoekstra* v *HM Advocate (No 3)* (2000) arose from an appeal against conviction on drug offences by four men. The men appealed to the High Court of Justiciary, to a Bench of three judges chaired by

Lord McCluskey. A devolution issue was raised on the ground that the court was not impartial as Lord McCluskey had expressed very strong disapproval of the European Convention on Human Rights in a series of newspaper articles. Leave to appeal to the Privy Council was refused and the men appealed against this decision. The appeal was therefore referred to a differently constituted Bench.

In criminal cases, the impartiality of the proceedings may be called into question if there is evidence of bias among the jury, as in the case of *Sander* v *United Kingdom* (2000). Sander, an Asian, was convicted of conspiracy to defraud. The trial had been adjourned following a complaint by a juror of racist comments from two other jury members. The judge redirected the jury but chose not to discharge them. The European Court of Human Rights held that there had been a breach of Art 6(1).

Access to justice

Article 6 contains no express right of access to a court but in *Golder* v *United Kingdom* (1979–80) the European Court held that it would be inconceivable that Art 6 should describe in detail the procedural guarantees afforded to parties in the course of litigation and should not first protect that which makes it possible to benefit from such guarantees, namely access to a court. In *Ashingdane* v *United Kingdom* (1985) the Court ruled that the right of access to the courts is not absolute but may be subject to limitations. In laying down regulations which limit access to courts, the Contracting States enjoy a margin of appreciation. Access to justice may involve resolution of disputes by other means, such as hearings before administrative tribunals or even consideration by an individual minister. The fairness of the procedure is more important than the status of the body making the decision.

In *W* v *United Kingdom* (1987) it was held that there had been a breach of Art 6 as the procedures for parents to appeal against the decisions of local authorities were inadequate. What was required by Art 6(1) was that parents must be able to have the decision taken by a local authority reviewed by a tribunal with jurisdiction to examine the merits of the matter. The powers of the courts in the United Kingdom did not extend to this and a breach of Art 6(1) had occurred.

There are two aspects to the principle that everyone is entitled to a right to a hearing:

- reasonable notice of the case against him;
- opportunity to make submissions to the hearing and to bring evidence to it.

Statutory exclusion of judicial control

Statutory provisions that prevent or restrict legal challenge by affected individuals are known as ouster clauses. The courts have always given the narrowest possible interpretation to ouster clauses, although they have been obliged to give effect to them where they are clear and unambiguous. The impact of Art 6(1) in this area is likely to be significant. For example, in the case of *Wilson* v *First County Trust Ltd (No 2)* (2001) the Court considered whether the restrictions on enforcement under the Consumer Credit Act 1974, s 127(3) infringed the company's human rights. The Act provided that a lender cannot enforce repayment of a loan where the loan agreement was defective in form. The Court granted a declaration of incompatibility on the basis that enforcement should be allowed were there had been no unfairness to the debtor. In *Hatton* v *United Kingdom* (2003), Mrs Hatton brought an application against the UK Government as she had suffered loss of sleep caused by night flights in and out of Heathrow airport. She was unable to bring a claim for damages for nuisance because s 76 of the Civil Aviation Act 1982 provided statutory immunity from such actions. She and other applicants were awarded damages of £4,000 each.

Legal aid

Legal aid is a system whereby financial assistance is provided to enable persons to secure legal advice and representation. Legal aid is widely available in relation to criminal prosecutions but its availability in relation to civil matters is more restricted. In *Airey* v *Ireland (No 1)* (1979–80), the European Court of Human Rights interpreted Art 6 to the effect that cases which affect an individual's civil rights should attract legal assistance in certain circumstances.

These circumstances include:

- the complexity of the case;
- the need for expert witnesses to establish facts; and
- the degree of emotional involvement of the applicant in the case.

Part 3 of the Convention Rights (Compliance) (Scotland) Act 2001 extends advice and assistance and civil legal aid to cases where Art 6 is likely to require it.

Public hearings

The right to a hearing in public is the only part of Art 6(1) that is not unqualified. Exclusions may take place for the following purposes:

- in the interests of morals, public order or national security in a democratic society;
- where the interests of juveniles or the protection of the private life of the parties so require; or
- to the extent strictly necessary in the opinion of the court in special circumstances where publicity would prejudice the interests of justice.

Trial within a reasonable time

Article 6(1) is not concerned with the need for a prompt trial where a person has been deprived of their personal liberty while awaiting a criminal trial. This is dealt with in Art 5. Article 6 is more concerned with a general principle of prompt administration of justice. In civil proceedings the reasonable time referred to in Art 6(1) normally refers to the elapsed time from the moment the action was instituted before the tribunal until the remedy is provided (*Poiss* v *Austria* (1987)). In criminal cases the relevant time begins when the person is officially notified that they have committed a criminal offence by a competent authority (*Dyer* v *Watson* (2001)). In *HM Advocate* v *P* (2001) two boys, aged 13 years, were indicted for the rape of a 14-year-old girl with learning difficulties. The rape allegedly took place on 11 March 1999 and the accused were charged on 16 March 1999. The case was allocated for trial on 19 February 2001. The boys claimed successfully that this was an unreasonable delay and breached Art 6(1).

The criteria for determining whether a delay is reasonable were considered by the European Court of Human Rights in the case of *Pailot* v *France* (2000). Pailot was a haemophiliac who brought an action for damages because he had been infected with the HIV virus by blood transfusion. His case was resolved by a friendly settlement, although the process took 3 years. It was held that, in assessing whether the length of proceedings exceeded a reasonable time, consideration had to be given to:

- the state of the proceedings at the start of the period under consideration;
- the nature and complexity of the dispute;
- the conduct of the parties; and
- the seriousness of the case.

It was held that the long delay in Pailot's case was not justified and amounted to breach of Art 6.

Where a case is complex and the interests of justice require that extended investigations are necessary, a longer period of delay will be deemed to be reasonable than in more straightforward cases. Delay may also be justified where the investigations are protracted because of technical considerations. This was held to be the case in *Crummock (Scotland) Ltd* v *HM Advocate* (2000). Contractors, while resurfacing a road, had allowed diesel oil to escape from a bowser and pollute the water supply to parts of Edinburgh. The environment agency initially investigated and informed Crummock that the case would not be referred to the fiscal. A year later an indictment was served on Crummock. He argued that there was a breach of Art 6(1) as the indictment was not served within a reasonable time and no explanation was given for the delay. It was held that, as it was a scientifically complex case, the delay was not so unreasonable as to contravene Art 6(1).

Equality of arms

The principle of equality of arms is that there must be a fair balance between the parties. It applies in both civil and criminal proceedings. It is more important that both parties are treated fairly than that a particular type of procedure should exist.

Legal representation

There is no right to legal representation; however, there could be a breach of Art 6 if the circumstances in which legal representation was provided, or not provided, favoured one party. In *McLean* v *Procurator Fiscal* (2001) it was argued that the regulations fixing the payment of solicitors under the legal aid system were in breach of the principle of equality of arms. This argument was rejected as the fact that defence solicitors were being paid a smaller fee should not mean that they would be ineffective.

Disclosure of evidence

In *Sinclair* v *HM Advocate* (2005), it was held that the prosecution is under a duty to disclose to the defence all material in its possession for or against the accused. This may include information which would undermine the case for the prosecution. The only grounds on which evidence can be withheld is where this is required on public interest grounds (eg to safeguard national security). It is important that any decision to withhold evidence is subject to judicial scrutiny. Such claims are referred to as public interest immunity. Information must only be withheld so far as it is necessary to protect the public interest and must never prejudice the overall fairness of the trial. In *R v H* (2004), a case involving an appeal against a conviction for conspiracy to supply drugs, the House of Lords held that public interest immunity was not a matter where a rigid set of rules would be appropriate. The matter should be decided on a case-by-case basis. The court should address a series of questions and, if careful attention was given to the questions and the proper interests of the defendant, there would be no violation of Art 6.

Questions to be addressed	Answer	Outcome
1 What is the material which the prosecution seeks to withhold?		Clarity about details
2 Is the material such as may weaken the prosecution case or strengthen that of the defence?	NO	Disclosure should not be ordered
	YES	Full disclosure should be ordered. (subject to 3, 4 and 5 below)
3 Is there a risk of serious prejudice to a specified important public interest if full disclosure is ordered ?	NO	Full disclosure should be ordered
	YES	See below
4 If the answer to 2 and 3 above is YES, can the defendant's interest be protected without disclosure?	YES	Disclosure should not be ordered
5 If the answer to 2, and 3 above is YES, can the defendant's interest be protected without disclosure?	NO	Disclosure short of full disclosure may be the solution
6 Will limited disclosure be unfair to the defendant?	NO	Only limited disclosure is needed
	YES	Fuller disclosure should be ordered (even if this means that the prosecution then abandons the case to avoid having to make a disclosure)
7 If the answer to 6 was NO, have circumstances changed as evidence unfolds during the trial?	YES	The court should keep its decision under review and change it if circumstances require it

Presumption of innocence

The right not to incriminate oneself is an element of the presumption of innocence but there may be circumstances when it will not be unfair to a person to seek and then use an admission of guilt. In *Brown* v *Stott* (2001), a person who had been accused of driving while intoxicated admitted to the police that she had been driving. It was held that there was no unfairness to the accused in allowing this admission to be used in the trial. There was a strong public interest in detecting and prosecuting road traffic offences and under Scots law there had to be corroborating evidence to show beyond all reasonable doubt that she committed the offence. Obtaining a confession by oppression will be a breach of Art 6. It was held in *R* v *Mushtaq* (2005) that a jury should be directed to ignore any confession that had been obtained by oppression.

In *R* v *DPP, ex parte Kebilene* (2000), Lord Hope considered the circumstances in which the burden of proof, which under Art 6 is with the prosecution, can shift to the accused. Statutory presumptions which place an evidential burden on the accused, requiring the accused to do no more than raise a reasonable doubt on the matter with which they deal, do not breach the presumption of innocence and are not incompatible with Art 6(2). Statutory presumptions which transfer the burden of proving that he is innocent to the accused may breach Art 6, depending on the individual circumstances. In *Attorney General's Reference (No 4 of 2002)* (2004) the House of Lords considered s 11(1) of the Terrorism Act 2000, which made it an offence to belong to a proscribed organisation. Section 11(2) provided a defence if the accused could prove that the organisation was not proscribed on the last (or only) occasion when he became a member, and that he had not taken part in the activities of the organisation at any time while it was proscribed. The House of Lords concluded that s 11(2) imposed a legal burden on the accused in breach of the presumption of innocence, that it was for a legitimate purpose of deterring people from joining terrorist organisations, but that it was not a proportionate response to the problem in the circumstances.

Article 6(3) sets out minimum rights for everyone charged with a criminal offence. The first of these is the right to be informed promptly, in a language which he understands and in detail, the nature and cause of the accusation against him. The second is the right to have adequate time and facilities for the preparation of a defence. An example of a breach of this Article would be a failure to allow a person in custody to have reasonable access to a lawyer. The third provision is that everyone charged with a criminal offence has the right to defend himself in person or through legal assistance of his own choosing, or to be given it free when the interests of justice so require. The three rights are not alternatives. A person cannot be forced to defend himself. Free legal assistance must be available for people charged with criminal offences who do not have funds to pay for a lawyer. The fourth right is to examine and cross-examine witnesses against him and to obtain the attendance and examination of witnesses on his behalf under the same conditions as witnesses against him. Finally, Art 6(3)(e) gives the right to have the free assistance of an interpreter if the accused cannot understand or speak the language used in court.

Frequently Asked Questions

What are the aspects of criminal legal procedure in Scotland which are likely to be challenged under Art 5?

One area which may be challenged is the lack of legal representation at the time of the police interview with the suspect. A person in custody has a right to have a lawyer informed of his arrest but there is no legal right under Scots law that a lawyer has to be present when an adult suspect is being questioned, merely that legal counsel is informed of a person's arrest. In *Paton* v *Ritchie* (2000) and *McLean* v *HM Advocate* (2009) it was held that the provision in Scots law, that a lawyer need not be present at all times when the accused is in communication with the police during detention, is not necessarily in contravention of Convention rights.

What is the difference between arrest and detention?

This is an issue that often causes confusion. In Scotland, the terms arrest and detention have different meanings. There is no statutory definition of detention in Scotland but it has been described as a form of limited or temporary arrest. Detention can range from stopping a person in the street for a few minutes to taking them into custody in a police station. Arrest is a formal process of taking a person into custody on being charged with an offence. In Scots law there are very specific rules relating to the rights of people who have been detained and who have been arrested. Under Art 5, the term detention is used to encompass both arrest and detention for the purpose of criminal investigation and other sorts of detention, such as detention of person with certain mental illnesses and detention of patients in hospitals to prevent the spread of disease.

Is the withholding of essential evidence on grounds of public interest immunity a breach of Art 6?

If the proper interests of the defendant are balanced against the importance to national security of withholding the evidence, there would be no violation of Art 6. It is a complex matter to be considered on a case-by-case basis. It is important that only information which is seriously prejudicial to the interests of national security should be withheld.

Essential Facts

Right to liberty

- Everyone "shall be entitled to trial within a reasonable time" and be "entitled to take proceedings by which the lawfulness of his detention shall be decided speedily by a court and his release ordered if the detention is not lawful".

- As it is a procedural right, the circumstances in which a person may be deprived of his liberty are limited to the 15 grounds set out in the six sub-paragraphs of the Article:

  - detention after conviction by a competent court;
  - non-compliance with the lawful order of a court;
  - in order to secure the fulfilment of any obligation prescribed by law;
  - on reasonable suspicion of having committed an offence;
  - when it is reasonably considered necessary to prevent his committing an offence;
  - to prevent a suspect fleeing after committing an offence;
  - detention of a minor by lawful order for the purpose of educational supervision;
  - detention of a minor to bring him before the competent legal authority;
  - prevention of the spreading of infectious diseases;
  - persons of unsound mind;
  - alcoholics;
  - drug addicts;
  - vagrants;
  - illegal immigrants;
  - persons awaiting deportation or extradition.

- The terms "arrest" and "detention" are interchangeably used in the text of Art 5.
- The UK Government (2001–08) sought derogations from Art 5 on grounds of the threat from Islamic terrorism in various aspects of its anti-terrorist legislation.

Right to a fair hearing

- Article 6(1) applies to civil rights and obligations as well as criminal charges. The term "civil rights and obligations" has an autonomous meaning and does not include ordinary private law disputes.
- Everyone is entitled to a fair hearing before an impartial and independent tribunal.
- Impartiality has two aspects:
  - an unbiased judge;
  - procedures that are fair for both parties.
- The emphasis on the need for independence produced some significant cases, followed by legislation to ensure that procedures for appointing judges are compatible with Art 6.
- Confiscation orders are not criminal charges but civil proceedings.

Essential Cases

De Wilde, Ooms and Versup v Belgium (1971): voluntary detention may still be unlawful.

Riera Blume v Spain (1999): positive obligation on state to protect individuals from others; members of a cult imprisoned by their families.

Murray v United Kingdom (1994): provided that the suspicion for detention is genuine, and the police officers concerned had reasonable suspicion, the detention will be lawful.

Winterwerp v Netherlands (1979): three criteria for the lawful detention of a person of unsound mind.

Anderson v Scottish Ministers (2002): challenge to the validity of the Mental Health, Public Safety and Appeals (Scotland) Act 1999.

Fox, Campbell and Hartley v United Kingdom (1990): an individual suspected by the police of a criminal offence must be told the "essential legal and factual grounds for his arrest".

Brogan v United Kingdom (1989): suspected IRA terrorists – 4 days and 6 hours pre-trial detention was too long.

A v Secretary of State for the Home Department (2004): declaration of incompatibility for s 23 of the Anti-terrorism, Crime and Security Act 2001.

Starrs v Ruxton (2000): right to a hearing before an impartial tribunal – temporary sheriffs not independent.

Clancy v Caird (No 1) (2000): right to a hearing before an impartial tribunal – temporary judges are independent.

Clark v Kelly (2001): independence of JPs in district courts.

Hoekstra v HM Advocate (No 3) (2000): bias – opinion of judge.

5 QUALIFIED RIGHTS

The qualified rights are the right to respect for private and family life, one's home and correspondence, the right to freedom of thought, conscience and religion, to freedom of expression and to freedom of assembly and association. They are open to greater flexibility by the parties to the European Convention on Human Rights. They are expressed in two parts. The first part defines the right conferred on the individual and the second part is a restricting clause setting out the public interest matters which would amount to a legitimate purpose for the state to restrict the right within its jurisdiction. The list of legitimate purposes for the restriction of the right is similar for each of the four rights; however, the list is not identical in each case. Article 9 lists only four legitimate aims whereas Art 10 lists nine, giving more scope for restrictions under domestic law.

Legitimate purpose	Art 8	Art 9	Art 10	Art 11
The interests of public safety	Yes	Yes	Yes	Yes
The protection of public order	Yes	Yes	Yes	Yes
The protection of health or morals	Yes	Yes	Yes	Yes
The protection of the rights and freedoms of others	Yes	Yes	Yes	Yes
The interests of national security	Yes		Yes	Yes
The economic well-being of the country	Yes			
The prevention of crime	Yes		Yes	Yes
Territorial integrity			Yes	
Protection of the reputation of others			Yes	
Preventing the disclosure of information received in confidence			Yes	
Maintaining the authority and impartiality of the judiciary			Yes	
The imposition of lawful restrictions on the exercise of these rights by members of the armed forces, of the police, or of the administration of the state.				Yes

An interference with a qualified right will not amount to a breach of the Convention provided that the restrictions meet the following four criteria:

- it must be lawful;
- it must be intended to pursue a legitimate purpose;
- it must be "necessary in a democratic society"; and
- it must not be discriminatory.

The process of judicial reasoning by which claims for the infringement of a qualified right are considered is as follows.

Question to consider	Answer	Outcome
1 Does the complaint fall within the rights protected by the Article?	No Yes	Application is not admissible Next question is considered
2 Is there an infringement of the right?	No Yes	Case is not upheld Next question is considered
3 Is the infringement according to law (ie is there an identifying legal authority for the act or decision)?	No Yes	Case is upheld Next question is considered
4 Is the infringing legal rule intended to achieve one of the legitimate aims stated in part 2 of the Article?	No Yes	Case is upheld Next question is considered
5 Were the measures taken necessary in a democratic society (ie proportionate to the legitimate aim to be achieved)?	No Yes	Case is upheld The infringement is justified; next question is considered
6 Was there any discrimination against the victim in the exercise of the right?	No Yes	The infringement is justified and no remedy is granted A remedy may be granted with respect to the discrimination

In practice, the judges do not stop their deliberations once one of the questions has been answered in a way which seals the outcome of the case. They will give a full judgment on all of the issues before the court.

There are also some preliminary conditions to be satisfied: the applicant, for example, must establish that he has been a victim of the infringement of the right.

If the complaint falls within the scope of a qualifying right but there is no existing protection in the specific circumstances under Scots or UK law, then there is a right to seek a remedy against the United Kingdom Government under Art 13 before the European Court of Human Rights.

RIGHT TO RESPECT FOR PRIVATE AND FAMILY LIFE, ONE'S HOME AND CORRESPONDENCE

Article 8 states:

"1 Everyone has the right to respect for his private and family life, his home and his correspondence.

2 There shall be no interference by a public authority with the exercise of this right except such as is in accordance with the law and is necessary in a democratic society in the interests of national security, public safety or the economic well-being of the country, for the prevention of disorder or crime, for the protection of health or morals, or for the protection of the rights and freedoms of others."

This Article protects the rights of the individual in two distinct ways. He or she is entitled to respect for his private life and relationships. He or she is also entitled to privacy and non-intervention by the state.

Respect for private life

The European Court of Human Rights has been unwilling to lay down a definitive interpretation of the concept of private life, preferring to leave it open to interpretation to meet the needs of individual circumstances. In *Niemietz* v *Germany* (1993) it was stated, with regard to the concept of family life, that:

"it would be too restrictive to limit the notion to an 'inner circle' in which the individual may live his own personal life as he chooses and to exclude therefrom entirely the outside world not encompassed within that circle. Respect for family life must also comprise to a certain degree the right to establish and develop relationships with other human beings".

It was also made clear in that judgment that private life could include business or professional activities engaged in by an individual. The right to respect for private life also includes the right to live in a manner suited to one's own personal beliefs and inclinations.

Positive obligation

There will be interference with private and family life whenever state action has a direct impact on an individual: for example, when property is searched. Article 8, however, has come to be regarded as requiring more from the states than that they should simply refrain from interfering with the private lives of citizens without justification. The notion of respect for privacy may be interpreted as including a positive obligation on the state to ensure that the privacy of the individual is protected. A state may be in contravention of Art 8 if it does not provide adequate legal safeguards to protect the privacy of individuals through measures such as data protection legislation. Data protection laws regulating the ways in which people can find out what information is being held about them by public authorities and commercial organisations are an important element of the protection of rights under Art 8. In the United Kingdom the process of collecting, storing, processing and distributing information is regulated by the Data Protection Act 1998. The Act protects the right to privacy by giving rights to individuals to find out what information is being held about them by organisations. The Act places obligations on those who record and use personal data (data users).

Scots law does not recognise a right of privacy *per se*, although the privacy of the home is protected by regulation of the police powers of entry and search. The Calcutt Report noted that a common law right to privacy could possibly develop in Scotland where there is a more general concept of *culpa* (legal wrong) in comparison with the more narrowly drawn English torts. There may be situations where the publication of private information may be restrained: for example, under Press Codes of Practice; publication of information may be prevented where it has been obtained in breach of confidence (*Quilty* v *Windsor* (1999)). The English case of *Douglas* v *Hello! Ltd* (2001) was brought by the actor Michael Douglas against *Hello!* magazine to prevent the magazine publishing pictures of his wedding to Catherine Zeta-Jones. Michael Douglas had entered into an exclusive contract with *OK* magazine for the rights to images of the wedding. *OK* argued that publication of the photographs by *Hello!* would amount to a breach of confidence. It was held that, by virtue of the Human Rights Act 1998, s 12(3), it was likely that Douglas would be able to establish that *Hello!* should not be allowed to publish the photographs because *Hello!* had breached the Code of Practice of the Press

Complaints Commission 1997. The issue was complicated by the fact that Michael Douglas had already sold his privacy for commercial gain and the current case was really no more than a dispute between two competing commercial interests. In his judgment Lord Justice Sedley concluded that a right of privacy between individuals should now be recognised as well as between public authorities and individuals. He said:

"What a concept of privacy does, however, is accord recognition to the fact that the law has to protect not only those people whose trust has been abused but those who simply find themselves subjected to an unwarranted intrusion into their personal lives. The law no longer needs to construct an artificial relationship of confidentiality between intruder and victim: it can recognise privacy itself as a legal principle drawn from the fundamental value of personal autonomy."

In *Campbell* v *Mirror Group Newspapers* (2004) the supermodel Naomi Campbell brought a breach of confidence action when photographs were published of her leaving a narcotics anonymous meeting. It was held that the publication of her photograph was a breach of privacy but the publication of the written information was justified in the public interest because she had made public statements that she did not take drugs. The public were entitled to know the truth. In *Mosley* v *News Group* (2008) the newspaper argued that there had been a public interest in publishing a story about the sadomasochistic sexual activities of Max Mosley as there had been Nazi concentration camp themes. The court held that the activities were not illegal but even if they had been it would not automatically justify publication on public interest grounds. Public interest was not established and the invasion of privacy was not justified.

The Press Complaints Commission's Code of Practice provides that everyone is entitled to respect for his private life, home, health and correspondence but publication is justified where it is in the public interest. Public interest is defined as including the detection of crime, the protection of public health and safety and preventing the public from being misled by a statement or action by an individual or organisation. The Press Complaints Commission qualifies as a public authority in terms of the Human Rights Act 1998 and is therefore obliged to have regard to Convention jurisprudence in adjudicating complaints.

The concept of private life encompasses the physical and moral integrity of the person, including his sexual life. In the case of *Dudgeon* v *United Kingdom* (1982) it was held that legislation in Northern Ireland which criminalised homosexual activities between consenting adult males was in breach of Art 8. In Scotland, Pt 4 of the Convention Rights (Compliance) (Scotland) Act 2001 provides that it is not an offence for more than two adult males to take part in homosexual acts in private. Activities will not be deemed to be in private where they take place in a public lavatory or other place to which the public has access. Investigations into the private lives of service personnel came under scrutiny in the case of *Smith* v *United Kingdom* (1999). Several service men and women sought compensation after they had been dismissed from the armed forces on the grounds of their sexual orientation. All four applicants contended that the investigations into their private lives by the Ministry of Defence constituted an infringement of their right to respect for their private lives under Art 8. The investigations had included detailed interviews with them and with their partners on matters relating to their sexual orientation and practices. The European Court of Human Rights held that the investigations, interviews and discharges amounted to an exceptional intrusion into the applicants' private lives, constituting a violation of Art 8. As a consequence of this decision the ban on homosexuals in the armed forces was lifted.

Respect for family life

The concept of family life is not restricted to situations where there is a traditional family in which the parents are married to each other. It is the right to live as a family or to have personal relationships which the Convention aims to protect. In *McMichael* v *United Kingdom* (1995) the parents of a young child, who were not married at the time of his birth, complained that their rights under Art 8 had been violated when they had been denied access to social reports, during care proceedings in respect of the child, who had been taken into care. Children's hearings took a number of decisions concerning custody and access arrangements and eventually freed the child for adoption. The parents had married by this time. The European Court of Human Rights held that Art 8 had been violated as there was evidence that the parents led a joint family life and acted together in their efforts to gain custody of the child.

In *R* v *Secretary of State for Health, ex parte L(M)* (2001), a convicted prisoner serving a life sentence applied for judicial review of a rule which restricted visits by his nephews until a risk assessment had been carried out. It was held that restrictions on child visits to patients at high security prisons were wholly justified and compatible with Art 8.

The closure of a home for severely disabled people was held to contravene Art 8 in the case of *R* v *North and East Devon HA, ex parte*

Coughlan (2000). Coughlan had been told that Mardon House would be a permanent home for her. It was held by the Court of Appeal that the decision to close Mardon House was in breach of Art 8 and also of a legitimate expectation brought about by the health authority's own promise. The closure decision was unfair and could not be justified by an overriding public interest.

The rights of the fathers of children who are the subjects of adoption orders have been considered in a number of cases since the implementation of the Human Rights Act 1998. The procedures followed in relation to adoption may amount to a breach of Art 8 if the rights of all of the family members are not respected. In *White* v *White* (2001), a husband appealed to the Inner House against the sheriff principal's decision to allow an appeal by his ex-wife, against an award of contact in his favour in respect of their youngest child. The husband argued that, under Art 8, interference with access between him and the child had to correspond with a pressing social need and be proportionate to the aim pursued. It was held that courts should have regard to the general principle that it was conducive to the welfare of children if their absent parents maintained contact with them on a regular basis as long as it was in the child's interest. In making regard for the child's welfare paramount, Scots law was in conformity with the approach laid down by the European Court.

In *Glaser* v *United Kingdom* (2000), the European Court held that Art 8 includes a positive obligation upon states to enable contact between a divorced or separated parent and his children. There is a right for a parent to have measures taken with a view to his being reunited with the child and an obligation for the national authorities to take such measures. This applies not only to cases dealing with the compulsory taking of children into public care, but also to cases where contact and residence disputes concerning children arise between parents and/ or other members of the children's family. The obligation to facilitate access is not absolute. The rights and freedoms of all concerned must be taken into account, and more particularly the best interest of the child and his rights under Art 8. In the *Glaser* case, the Court concluded that the English and Scottish authorities had achieved a fair balance between the competing interests of the applicant, his ex-wife and their children.

When citizens of different countries marry, it goes without saying that they wish to live together as a family. One of the barriers to this is the fact that the right to live in a country depends on the laws of the country concerned. Immigration into Scotland is a matter of UK law. Infringement of Art 8 is frequently raised as a ground of challenge where one spouse is being denied leave to enter or where a parent is facing deportation.

Ahmed, Petitioner (2000) was a case in which a Pakistani citizen sought judicial review of a decision to refuse to grant him leave to enter the United Kingdom. He had married a UK citizen after action had been taken against him in relation to immigration. It was argued successfully that Art 8 of the European Convention on Human Rights does not confer an unrestricted right to enter or remain in a country. The duty imposed by Art 8 cannot be considered as amounting to a general obligation on the part of a state to respect the choice made by married couples of the country of their matrimonial residence and to accept the non-national spouse for settlement in that country. There are provisions within the Immigration Rules for a person to enter as the spouse of a British citizen or person settled here, if the criteria set out within the Rules are met. In the *Ahmed* case the rules had not been met as the marriage had taken place after action had been instigated against Ahmed. There was no breach of Art 8.

The threat of deportation may involve a difficult choice for the family of the person being deported. The family could remain in the United Kingdom or leave with the person being deported. The attitude of the courts is that a decision to deport a parent is not necessarily an infringement of the right to respect for family life as the family is also free to leave. Exceptions may be made where the applicant's family ties with the country are long established, as in *Mehemi* v *France* (2000). Mehemi was an Algerian national, who was born in France in 1962 and lived there until his deportation in 1995 following his conviction for drug trafficking. In addition to his parents and siblings, some of whom were French nationals, he also left behind his wife, resident in France since 1978, and their three children, who were all French nationals. Mehemi complained that his permanent exclusion had interfered with his right to family life, contrary to Art 8(2). The complaint was allowed as Mehemi had shown that his established French private life had been interfered with by the order. The use of deportation in such cases had to strike a balance between crime prevention and the preservation of public order, and the individual's rights under Art 8.

Respect for one's home

In *Buckley* v *United Kingdom* (1996), the UK Government asserted that the term "home" only applied to a residence which had been legally established according to national law. The applicant was a gypsy who had bought a piece of land and then lived on it with her family in three caravans for a number of years. She applied for planning permission to build a house but permission was refused and enforcement proceedings were taken to remove the caravans. The Court decided that the caravans were her home. It was held, however, that the interference with her home was justified in this case, as it was necessary for the economic well-being of the country and for the protection of the health and rights of other persons.

States can be held liable under Art 8 for causing, or failing to prevent, environmental pollution which interferes with a person's right to respect for their home. In *Lopez Ostra* v *Spain* (1994), the applicant claimed that her rights under Art 8 had been infringed by pollution. A tannery reprocessing plant had been built, close to her flat. This caused adverse effects on the health of the family and they had to move. The Court held that severe environmental pollution could interfere with the right to respect for a person's home. The state argued that the interference was justified in the interests of the economic well-being of the area but the Court held that the state had not achieved a fair balance between the interests of the community and the rights of the applicant. It was held that there was a breach of Art 8 and damages were awarded.

Noise and disruption from neighbours is another area where it could be argued that the state should be aware of this positive obligation. In recent years the law in Scotland has responded to this issue and local authorities now have two specific powers that enable them to protect the right of the citizen to peaceful enjoyment of his home. Potentially, a failure by a local authority to exercise these powers could lead to a challenge under the Human Rights Act 1998 by a person whose private home life is disrupted by the conduct of neighbours. Anti-social behaviour orders under the Crime and Disorder Act 1998, s 19 are intended to protect persons in the authority's area from further anti-social acts or conduct by an individual. Local authorities also have specific powers arising from their role as landlords: for example, the Crime and Disorder Act 1998, s 23 entitles a local authority to terminate a secure tenancy if the behaviour of people at the house interferes with the rights of neighbours.

Respect for one's correspondence

The interception of communications is permitted in a wide range of circumstances. There must, however, be clear, specific unambiguous legal authority for any invasion of privacy. In *Klass* v *Germany* (1979–80), the Court held that the interception of postal and telephone communications in national security cases was consistent with Art 8 where it was necessary in the interests of national security or for the prevention of disorder or crime and there were controls and safeguards sufficient to prevent abuse. In *Malone* v *United Kingdom* (1984) it was held that Art 8 had been violated by intercepting telephone conversations without specific legal authorisation. The law regarding interception of communications was unclear at the time. The interception, acquisition and disclosure of communications data is now regulated by the Regulation of Investigatory Powers Acts.

Whether the law should protect the interception of communications within private premises was considered in the case of *Halford* v *United Kingdom* (1997). Telephone conversations of Alison Halford, Assistant Chief Constable in Merseyside, were intercepted by senior officers. She applied to the European Court of Human Rights, alleging a breach of Art 8. It was ruled that the Convention had been violated and she was awarded compensation of £10,000. The Court stated that it is clear that telephone calls made from business premises as well as from the home may be covered by the notions of "private life" and "correspondence" within the meaning of Art 8. There was no evidence of any warning being given to Ms Halford, as a user of the internal telecommunications system, that calls made on the system would be liable to interception. She would have a reasonable expectation of privacy for her calls. The Court stated:

> "In the context of secret measures of surveillance or interception of communications by public authorities, because of the lack of public scrutiny and the risk of misuse of power, the domestic law must provide some protection to the individual against arbitrary interference with Article 8 rights. Thus, the domestic law must be sufficiently clear in its terms to give citizens an adequate indication as to the circumstances and conditions on which public authorities are empowered to resort to any such secret measures."

In the case of correspondence of prisoners it may be difficult to balance the rights of the individual to privacy for his correspondence and the legitimate aim of preventing crime. In *Campbell* v *United Kingdom* (1992) the letters of a prisoner serving a life sentence in Scotland were opened and read by prison authorities. The correspondence included letters from his solicitor and from the European Commission. The Court held that the opening of letters to Campbell had been in accordance with the law with a legitimate aim of preventing crime or disorder. However, correspondence between a lawyer and his client should only be opened when the authorities have reasonable grounds to suspect that the privilege is being abused and that the contents of a letter may endanger prison security or the safety of others. In the absence of such evidence, opening letters between a solicitor and his client is not necessary in a democratic society. There was no justification for letters from the Commission being opened. There had, therefore, been breaches of Art 8.

LEGITIMATE PURPOSES FOR INTERFERENCE WITH RIGHTS UNDER ART 8

Protection of public health and morals

The disclosure of medical records by state health authorities will amount to a breach of the right to respect for a person's private life but it may be justifiable if it is necessary to protect public health. In *Z* v *Finland* (1998) the applicant had been married to a man who had been charged with serious sexual offences. He was charged with attempted manslaughter on the ground that he had known that he was HIV positive at the time when he committed the offences. In order to find out when he knew that he was HIV positive, the court ordered Z's doctor to provide evidence about her health. He disclosed that she was HIV positive. The proceedings were held in private and records of the case were to be kept secret for 10 years. The man appealed and a copy of the appeal court judgment, which identified the applicant and disclosed her HIV status, was given to the press and published in several newspapers. The Court found that there had been a breach of Art 8.

Preventing disorder or crime

Police powers of search potentially breach Art 8 but are justified so far as is necessary for the legitimate purpose of preventing disorder or crime. Unless a person has been arrested there is no power to search them under common law. Evidence obtained from a search to which a person has voluntarily consented to be searched will, however, be admissible in a trial (*Devlin* v *Normand* (1992)). In situations of extreme urgency searches carried out before arrest may be excused and the evidence obtained may be used at trial. The decision to use the evidence must balance the public interest in the effective investigation of crime against the protection of the accused from arbitrariness, dishonesty or oppression. Search before arrest may be authorised by a specific statutory provision such as s 60 of the Civic Government (Scotland) Act 1982 which provides that a police constable has power to search a person suspected on reasonable grounds of being in possession of stolen property. Statutory powers of search must be exercised strictly in accordance with the procedures laid down by the relevant statute. Once they have been arrested, the police have a power at common law to search a person and to photograph them, to make a physical examination and to take fingerprints, palm prints or other such prints and impressions of an external part of the body. On the authority of an officer of the rank of inspector or above, a constable may take samples of hair, fingernail or toenail clippings or scrapings, a sample of blood or other body fluids, a sample of saliva or body tissue obtained from an external part of the body by means of swabbing or rubbing (Criminal Procedure (Scotland) Act 1995, as amended by the Police, Public Order and Criminal Justice (Scotland) Act 2006)).

Power of entry to premises

At common law a constable is justified in entering premises without a warrant only in certain limited circumstances. He can enter premises if he is in close pursuit of a person who has committed or attempted to commit a serious crime. Serious crimes include murder, rape, robbery, and theft by housebreaking. Several statutes authorise a police officer to enter premises without warrant. In each case the police may only take the specific actions which are authorised by the statute: for example, under the Licensing (Scotland) Act 1976 the police may enter licensed premises to investigate breaches of the licensing conditions.

In *McLeod* v *United Kingdom* (1999), following divorce proceedings the applicant had been ordered to give her husband furniture from the former matrimonial home, in which she lived with her mother. Thinking that she had agreed to allow him to collect the items, her husband arrived at the home accompanied by relatives and two police officers. Mrs McLeod's mother let Mr McLeod and his relatives into the house and they removed the furniture. The policemen then went into the house and checked the items taken against the list in the court order. The Court held that, as soon as it became apparent that Mrs McLeod was not at home, the policemen should not have entered the property, as there was no risk of a crime or disorder occurring. The Court held that the policemen's actions had been disproportionate to the legitimate aim and there had been a violation of Art 8.

Search of premises

The police may only search premises without a warrant if they have the full and free consent of the occupier of the premises or where a person has been arrested on a serious charge and a delay in carrying out a search may defeat the ends of justice. Searches of premises may also be carried out under specific statutory powers. The procedures by which warrants are granted came under scrutiny in the case of *Birse* v *HM Advocate* (2000).

Birse claimed that a search warrant issued under the Misuse of Drugs Act 1971, s 23(3) had violated his rights under Art 8. It was accepted that a search of a person's home was an interference with the right to respect for his home. However, provided that the search was conducted under a warrant, and the warrant was granted in accordance with s 23(2), then the search conducted under the warrant was in accordance with the law. It was also accepted that the purpose of the search was for the prevention of crime and that a warrant to search could be necessary in a democratic society for the purpose of preventing drugs offences.

Protection of national security

The protection of national security may require that a state keeps secret files about individuals. In *Leander* v *Sweden* (1987), the applicant was prevented from continuing his job at a naval museum after military authorities had been shown a secret file on him maintained by the National Police Board. It was held that both the storing and the release of such information amounted to an interference with Leander's private life as guaranteed by Art 8(1), the interference was no more than was necessary for the protection of national security, there were adequate procedural safeguards and so the requirements of Art 8(2) were satisfied.

In the United Kingdom, surveillance in the interests of national security may be carried out with lawful authority by two organisations. MI5 is the internal security service and MI6 deals with overseas security. The service is not accountable to local police authorities and the actions of its members may not be the subject of complaints under the police complaints procedures. Surveillance practices in the United Kingdom were considered by the Commission in *Hewitt* v *United Kingdom* (1992). The applicants had both worked for the National Council for Civil Liberties (now known as Liberty). They complained that the Security Service had kept files on them as "Communist sympathisers". A majority of the Commission gave the opinion that the Security Service had interfered with the applicants' private lives and was in breach of Art 8(1). The interference could not be brought within the exceptions in Art 8(2), because, at the relevant time, the Security Service did not have lawful authority for its actions. The Security Service Act 1989 subsequently provided the necessary lawful authority. The Intelligence Services Act 1994 established a Parliamentary Intelligence and Security Committee to scrutinise the work of the security services. The Regulation of Investigatory Powers Act and the Regulation of Investigatory Powers (Scotland) Act 2000 regulate surveillance with a stated aim to ensure that the exercise of these powers is compatible with the provisions of the Human Rights Act 1998. A general principle under the Acts is that surveillance will be authorised only if it is necessary and proportionate. The Acts deal with the regulatory framework of a range of investigatory powers including the interception, acquisition and disclosure of communications data, the use of covert and intrusive surveillance and of human intelligence gathering. However, the Acts have been challenged on the ground that they deprive people who suspect that they have been under surveillance from recourse to a remedy in the ordinary courts. The remedy is provided instead by a tribunal. The tribunal has jurisdiction in relation to matters covered by both Acts. The Act states that the jurisdiction of the tribunal shall be the only appropriate tribunal for the purposes of s 7 of the Human Rights Act 1998 (proceedings for actions incompatible with Convention rights). There is a time limit of 1 year for bringing complaints. The English Act gives a Minister power to authorise surveillance for any purpose specified by an order of a Minister. This "catch-all" section was not included in the Scottish Act as it was deemed by the Scottish Parliament to be unsuitable for modern day democracy.

Economic well-being of the country

In *Gillow* v *United Kingdom* (1986), an application was brought by a victim of a decision made to protect the economic well-being of the island of Guernsey. Mr and Mrs Gillow had moved to Guernsey in 1956 so that Mr Gillow could work there. They built a house and lived in it until 1960 when Mr Gillow took a job overseas. They did not sell the house but rented it. People could only live on Guernsey if they had a resident's licence. In 1979 the Gillows returned to Guernsey but were refused a resident's licence and had to sell the house and leave. It was held that the house in Guernsey was the Gillows' home. The fact that they were prevented from living in their home was an interference with their right to respect for their home. Although it was legitimate for the authorities to try to control the population of Guernsey so as to promote the economic well-being of the island, the action taken was disproportionate to that aim in the Gillows' case.

FREEDOM OF THOUGHT, CONSCIENCE AND RELIGION

Article 9 states:

> "1 Everyone has the right to freedom of thought, conscience and religion; this right includes freedom to change his religion or belief and freedom, either alone or in community with others and in public or private, to manifest his religion and belief, in worship,

teaching, practice and observance.

2 Freedom to manifest one's religion or beliefs shall be subject only to such limitations as are prescribed by law and are necessary in a democratic society in the interests of public safety, for the protection of public order, health or morals, or for the protection of the rights and freedoms of others."

There can be no doubt about the importance of this right, particularly when it is set in a historical and political context. Freedom of religious observance has been a matter of fundamental importance throughout Europe for several centuries. In the United Kingdom it has to be considered in the context of a multi-cultural society in which the Christian religion holds a dominant position and in which there is still a close link between the established church and the state.

Article 9 has three distinct elements: freedom of belief; right to act in accordance with the belief; and to do so collectively.

Freedom of belief

The Convention establishes an absolute right to freedom of thought, conscience and religion. The right is not limited to religious beliefs but can be applied equally to moral and political ideologies. It is unlikely that this right will come under any threat in the United Kingdom.

Right to act in accordance with the belief

Article 9 establishes a freedom, either alone or in community with others and in public or private, to manifest religion and belief, in worship, teaching, practice and observance. This right to carry out activities associated with religion and other beliefs distinguishes Art 9 from Art 10, which gives a right to express views and opinions. Article 9 can be seen as a limitation on the freedom of expression in that, in order to allow people to observe their religious beliefs without interference, it may be necessary to limit the freedom of expression of others (for example, by blasphemy laws). Thus, for example, it would not be contrary to Art 9 for a local authority to refuse permission to a religious group to hold a procession on the grounds that there is a strong risk of sectarian violence. In *X v United Kingdom* (1976) the Commission considered an application from a prisoner who had been refused permission to have a religious book in his cell. The book in question contained a section on martial arts. The prison authorities considered that this could be dangerous to the general prison population. It was held that the prisoner's right under Art 9(1) had been interfered with but that the interference was for the legitimate purposes of protecting public safety and public order. The action was not disproportionate to the purpose and so was justified in terms of Art 9(2).

Questions have arisen with regard to the activities which can be classified as manifestations of a belief. The Article itself specifies worship, teaching, practice and observance as manifestations of belief. In *C v United Kingdom* (1983) it was held that withholding a portion of income tax so as not to support the research and production of weapons did not qualify as a manifestation of belief. Consequently, action to enforce payment of the tax was not an interference with rights contrary to Art 9. In *Valsamis v Greece* (1997) Valsamis's parents, who were Jehovah's Witnesses, objected to Valsamis taking part in parades to celebrate National Day commemorating the outbreak of war between Greece and Italy. Valsamis's request to be excused attendance was refused but she did not take part in the school parade. She was suspended for one day. Her parents applied to the Commission in alleging breaches of the right to freedom of religion, contrary to Art 9. It was held that, since the obligation to take part in the school parade did not offend her parents' religious convictions, there was no breach of Art 9.

Collective right

Article 9 states that a person has freedom, either alone or in community with others and in public or private, to manifest his religion and belief. This gives collective rights in addition to individual rights. This means that the Convention right can be relied on by organisations representing people collectively, for example schools or charitable societies. In *Chappell v United Kingdom* (1990) the applicant was a practising druid who claimed that the ban on the summer solstice ceremony which had taken place at Stonehenge every year since 1917 was a breach of his rights under Art 9. It was held that the ban was lawful and was necessary in a democratic society for the purposes of protecting public order, protecting the rights and freedoms of others and in the interests of public safety.

Article 9 merits a specific provision in the Human Rights Act 1998. Section 13 states that "if a court's determination of any question arising under this Act might affect the exercise by a religious organisation (itself or its members collectively) of the Convention right to freedom of thought, conscience and religion, it must have particular regard to the importance of that right". Section 13 was inserted to meet concerns expressed by religious groups that one consequence of the Human Rights Act 1998 might be that the state would begin to interfere in matters of religious doctrine, for example by requiring churches to perform marriage ceremonies for homosexual couples. The direction that courts should have regard to the importance of the right is not intended to give any special status to Art 9 over and above any of the other rights. It is still open to a court to decide, for example, that the right of free expression under Art 10 takes precedence over rights under Art 9 in the circumstances under consideration at the time.

Article 9 does not give protection against discrimination on religious grounds. That is given by Art 14, but only in connection with other Convention rights. The case of *R* v *Chief Metropolitan Stipendiary Magistrate, ex parte Choudhury* (1991) was an application for judicial review of the refusal to grant a summons against the author Salman Rushdie for the offences of blasphemous libel and seditious libel. Rushdie had written a novel called *The Satanic Verses*, which Choudhury found offensive to Islam. The English common law offence of blasphemy was not applicable to Islam. Choudhury argued that blasphemy should be extended to cover Islam and that its failure to do so contravened the right to religious freedom guaranteed under the Convention. It was held that the fact that blasphemy did not apply to Islam did not mean that the United Kingdom was in breach of its responsibilities under the Convention.

A right not to hold religious beliefs

It was made clear in *Kokkinakis* v *Greece* (1994) that the protection afforded by Art 9 is not only protection for established, organised, traditional religions but also for the right to hold unconventional beliefs which are not shared by others. The Court said in that case: "... freedom of thought, conscience and religion is one of the foundations of a 'democratic society' within the meaning of the Convention. It is, in its religious dimension, one of the most vital elements that go to make up the identity of believers and their conception of life, but it is also a precious asset for atheists, sceptics and the unconcerned". In *Kokkinakis* v *Greece*, laws prohibiting attempts to persuade others to join a religious group were held to contravene Art 9. Jehovah's Witnesses who had been fined for entering people's homes and attempting to recruit new members applied successfully to the European Court of Human Rights. The Court held that freedom of religion includes the right to try to convince one's neighbour, provided that the means by which this is achieved are not improper. In the census of the UK population carried out in April 2001, people were asked, for the first time, whether they belonged to a religious organisation and, if so, which one. It was not compulsory to answer the question, but there was some disquiet in some sectors of the population about being asked.

FREEDOM OF EXPRESSION

Article 10 states:

> "1   Everyone has the right to freedom of expression. This right shall
>   include freedom to hold opinions and to receive and impart
>   information and ideas without interference by public authority
>   and regardless of frontiers. This Article shall not prevent States
>   from requiring the licensing of broadcasting, television or cinema
>   enterprises.
>
> 2   The exercise of these freedoms, since it carries with it duties and
>   responsibilities, may be subject to such formalities, conditions,
>   restrictions or penalties as are prescribed by law and are necessary
>   in a democratic society, in the interests of national security,
>   territorial integrity or public safety, for the prevention of disorder
>   or crime, for the protection of health or morals, for the protection
>   of the reputation or rights of others, for preventing the disclosure
>   of information received in confidence, or for maintaining the
>   authority and impartiality of the judiciary."

The wording of Art 10 suggests a relatively wide set of circumstances in
which freedom of expression may be restricted. The purposes of protection
of territorial integrity, protection of the reputation of others, preventing
the disclosure of information received in confidence and maintaining the
authority and impartiality of the judiciary are exclusive to this Article.
The general approach of the European Court of Human Rights in relation
to Art 10 is shown in the case of *Handyside* v *United Kingdom* (1979–80).
Handyside was a publisher who obtained the UK rights to publish a book
called *The Little Red Schoolbook*. It was written and published originally
in Denmark and had been published in several other European countries.
The book included a section on sex education. After review copies were
sent out, Handyside was charged in England with having an obscene
publication in his possession. He was fined and the books were forfeited.
(A prosecution in Scotland was unsuccessful.) The European Court of
Human Rights held that there had been no violation of Art 10. There
had been interference with his right to freedom of expression but the
interference was for the legitimate aim of protecting morals. In relation to
whether the action taken against Handyside was within the boundaries of
what is necessary in a democratic society, the Court held that the English
courts had not exceeded what was reasonably necessary in the context
of the views on ethics and education in the United Kingdom. The fact
that the book was published elsewhere without challenge was not an

argument which the Court could accept as a wide margin of appreciation was allowed in relation to freedom of expression.

Protecting democracy

Freedom of expression is an essential element of democracy. The ability of citizens to exercise informed choice between political parties depends on members of each party being free to publicise their views. Freedom of expression is also important in wider spheres of life. Scientific developments can be impeded by rules which suppress the sharing of ideas. Nevertheless, the right of one individual to express his views has to be balanced against the rights of others.

Before the Human Rights Act 1998 came into force, the right to freedom of expression enjoyed considerable protection under the common law and through a number of statutes. There are also a number of restrictions which are broadly compatible with the permitted restrictions under Art 10. In *BBC, Petitioners* (2000), the BBC petitioned the *nobile officium* of the Court of Session for consent to broadcast by television the proceedings in the Lockerbie trial. The BBC argued that, as the court had already given consent to broadcasting the trial by way of television to four remote sites, refusing to allow broadcasts to the general public breached its rights under the European Convention on Human Rights, Art 10. It was held that the restrictions were justified under Art 10(2).

The Human Rights Act 1998 has made special provision for freedom of expression. Section 12 provides:

> "if a court is considering whether to grant any relief which, if granted, might affect the exercise of the Convention right to freedom of expression, the court must have particular regard to the importance of the Convention right to freedom of expression and, where the proceedings relate to material which the respondent claims, or which appears to the court, to be journalistic, literary or artistic material (or to conduct connected with such material), the court must have regard to:
>
> (a) the extent to which –
>
>   (i) the material has, or is about to, become available to the public; or
>
>   (ii) it is, or would be, in the public interest for the material to be published;
>
> (b) any relevant privacy code."

The section is inspired by the purpose of ensuring freedom of the press. It was introduced as a result of concern expressed during the passage of the Act that the incorporation of the European Convention on Human Rights restricts press freedom. It will not be sufficient to show that the material is, for example, journalistic and that it is about a public figure; the court will need to look at the specific material and decide whether it should be published.

There will always be potential conflict between the rights to privacy under Art 8 and the rights to freedom of expression under Art 10. The Human Rights Act 1998 has not made freedom of expression an absolute right but it has created an obligation on the courts to give a high priority to freedom of expression. This does not mean that Art 10 will always override Art 8. The Act does direct that courts have regard to any privacy codes. This will include the codes of practice produced by self-regulatory bodies such as the Press Complaints Commission and the Broadcasting Standards Council.

LEGITIMATE PURPOSES FOR INTERFERENCE WITH RIGHTS UNDER ART 10

Protecting the reputation of others

Defamation

Provided that the restriction the law of defamation imposes on freedom of expression does not exceed that which is necessary in a democratic society, restrictions for this purpose will not contravene the Convention. The purpose of the law of defamation is to protect individuals against false statements, which may cause harm to their reputations and to provide a mechanism for compensation where such harm has occurred. The law of defamation has been criticised as providing inadequate protection for the individual from unwarranted intrusion by the press into private lives as the process of gaining compensation for defamatory remarks is expensive and slow.

The law of defamation could be a serious threat to free and open debate in the course of debates in Parliament and to judicial proceedings. For this reason, the protection of absolute privilege is given to:

- words spoken in proceedings in the Westminster Parliament (Bill of Rights 1689);
- statements in the course of judicial proceedings;

- statements made in the course of proceedings in the Scottish Parliament (Scotland Act 1998, s 41);
- publications made under the authority of the Westminster or Scottish Parliament, eg official reports of debates, committee papers and radio or television broadcasts of proceedings.

Absolute privilege means that whatever the accuracy of the statement or the intent with which it was made, no action for defamation can be based on it.

Qualified privilege is given to reports of Parliamentary or judicial proceedings. Qualified privilege applies where a statement is a fair and accurate report of the proceedings and it is made without malice (Defamation Act 1996, s 15).

Protection of morals

The laws which interfere with freedom of expression on the grounds of obscenity can be regarded as lawful in terms of Art 10(2) as being for the legitimate aim of protecting morals. Arguments in favour of restrictions tend to emphasise the need to protect members of society from corrupting influences. Definitions of obscenity depend on contemporary standards of decency, taste and morality. It is difficult to apply an objective standard of acceptability for publications. Some publications which were regarded as obscene as little as 40 years ago are considered acceptable today. Obscene publications are those which "possess the liability to corrupt and deprave those to whom they are sold and exposed" (*Ingram v Macari* (1983)).

The majority of cases involving obscene publications are heard before the courts in England and Wales because the majority of publishers are within the jurisdiction of the English courts. The control of obscene material is becoming increasingly difficult now that electronic communications and access to the internet make it possible for individuals to import material directly from outside the United Kingdom.

It is an offence under the Civic Government (Scotland) Act 1982, s 51 to display any obscene material in any public place, or in any other place where it can be seen by the public. Material is defined as any book, magazine, bill, paper, print, film, tape, disc or other kind of recording (whether of sound or visual images or both), photograph, drawing, painting, representation, model or figure. Performances of plays or television and radio broadcasting are not restricted by this section although they are subject to controls through the licensing system. Performances of films and video recordings are subject to a classification system. It is also an offence under the Civic Government (Scotland) Act 1982, s 51 to publish, sell or distribute any obscene material or to keep any obscene material with a view to its eventual sale or distribution.

Maintaining the authority and impartiality of the judiciary

The law of contempt is used to prevent publicity which may prejudice a trial both prior to and during the trial. Contempt of court is not strictly a crime but penalties may be imposed on a party in contempt. The law of contempt of court restricts freedom of expression, particularly on the part of newspaper journalists and radio and television broadcasters, by preventing the reporting of anything which could be prejudicial to court proceedings. Publication of matters which are in contempt of court is regulated by the Contempt of Court Act 1981. A publication is defined as including any speech, writing, broadcast or other communication in whatever form, which is addressed to the public at large or to a section of the public (s 2(1)). An example of the effect of the law of contempt on newspaper reporting was the case of *HM Advocate* v *News Group Newspapers* (1989). Following the shooting of a Yugoslavian in Kirkcaldy, two newspapers published articles of a fairly sensational nature relating to the incident. These articles were published the day after the shooting and subsequent arrest of a suspect, and the Lord Advocate presented petitions against both newspaper companies on the ground that the articles were in breach of the Contempt of Court Act 1981, s 2. Both newspapers were held to be in contempt of court. The article in one newspaper was fairly specific in its allegations, implying that the suspect was guilty but not naming him. A heavier fine was imposed on that newspaper. The 1981 Act lays down a rule of strict liability when court proceedings are active.

In Scotland, actions for contempt of court are usually brought by the Lord Advocate. They may also be brought by a party to a trial who considers that the course of justice will be impeded. An action for contempt of court may be brought by an accused person in a criminal trial. Fair and accurate reports of legal proceedings, held in public, and published contemporaneously and in good faith, do not attract the strict liability rule. In *HM Advocate* v *Danskin* (2000) a sheriff made an order under the Contempt of Court Act restricting reporting of proceedings until return of the jury's verdict. The press and media sought reduction of the order. It was held that it was necessary to balance Danskin's Convention rights under Art 6 and the rights of the press under Art 10. There was no substantial risk of prejudice to Danskin's right to a fair hearing if reporting was fair and accurate.

A publication which is a discussion in good faith of public affairs or matters of general public interest will not be held to be in contempt if the risk of impeding or prejudicing legal proceedings is merely incidental to the discussion. In the case of *HM Advocate* v *Scottish Media Newspapers Ltd* (2000) a television actor had been charged with threatening a sheriff officer with an axe. On the same date as his first court appearance, an article appeared in a newspaper stating that he had been arrested. The article also stated that the actor had a history of drink problems and that neighbours had complained about disturbances at his home. It was held that there was not a substantial risk of prejudice to the course of justice as the trial was unlikely to take place until more than 9 months after the article's publication and the court must assume that a jury would follow the judge's direction only to consider the evidence heard in court. In those circumstances it could not be said that the article was in contempt of court. In the case of the *Sunday Times* v *United Kingdom* (1979), the *Sunday Times* complained of a violation of the right to freedom expression under Art 10, when they were prevented from publishing an article which was critical of the Distillers drugs company during negotiations for compensation for victims of the drug thalidomide. The Court held that the interference with the right to freedom of expression was not necessary in a democratic society. There was no social need sufficiently pressing to outweigh the public interest in freedom of expression. The article contained information on a matter of undisputed public concern. Article 10 confers not only a right on the press to inform the public but also a right on the public to be informed.

Section 10 of the Contempt of Court Act 1981 regulates the disclosure of sources. The court may not require disclosure, and a person will not be guilty of contempt as a result of failure to disclose a source of information, unless the court is satisfied that "disclosure is necessary in the interests of justice or national security or for the prevention of disorder or crime". In *Goodwin* v *United Kingdom* (2002), Goodwin had been given information about the financial problems of a company called Tetra Ltd. Tetra obtained an injunction preventing publication. The High Court ordered Goodwin to identify the source of his information. He refused and was found guilty of contempt of court and fined £5,000. The European Court of Human Rights held that there was therefore an infringement of Art 10. This approach in the *Goodwin* case has now been followed in the post Human Rights Act 1998 case of *Ashworth Security Hospital* v *MGN Ltd* (2001). It was held that, in interpreting s 10 of the Contempt of Court Act, the courts in the United Kingdom should apply the same test of necessity as that applied by the European Court. In that case MGN, a newspaper group, appealed against an order that it disclose the identity of a person who had supplied information relating to a well-known offender from the database of a special security hospital. It was held that interference with the right to protect the source of information was justified in this case because the disclosure of confidential medical records to the press was misconduct which was contrary to the public interest.

The behaviour of people present at court hearings may also be restricted by the law of contempt of court. Anything which amounts to disrespectful words or conduct may be held by a judge to be contempt of court. An example of this type of contempt arose in the case of *Young* v *Lees* (1998). Young was present at the trial of his partner. When she was remanded in custody, Young shouted "You guffy" at the sheriff. The sheriff found him in contempt of court. He was sentenced to 60 days' imprisonment. The laws which confer such powers on members of the judiciary are for the purpose of maintaining the authority of the judiciary.

Protection of the rights and freedoms of others

Restrictions on freedom of political expression

Broadcasting during elections is controlled by ss 92 and 93 of the Representation of the People Act 1983. The purpose of the restrictions is to preserve equality between the candidates from different parties. In particular, the aim is to protect the rights of individuals or groups with limited financial resources. Expenditure on national party election broadcasts is met out of the central funds of each party. Party election broadcasts may only be made by the British Broadcasting Corporation and under the authority of the Independent Broadcasting Authority. Political advertising is not permitted on television or radio. If a candidate participates in a broadcast for the purpose of promoting his own election, every other candidate in the constituency must consent to the broadcast. No broadcast may be made without the consent of any candidate who appears in the programme. In *Marshall* v *BBC* (1979) an objection was raised because a candidate who had refused to take part in a broadcast was filmed while canvassing in the streets. It was held that the broadcast did not breach any regulation: to "take part" in a broadcast about a constituency means to take an active part in the programme.

Independent broadcasting authorities are under a duty under the Broadcasting Act 1990 to maintain accuracy and impartiality. Although direct television advertising by political parties is prohibited, each party is allowed a number of party political broadcasts. The amount of time allocated to each party is determined according to the proportion of the overall vote which the party secured at the previous election. This allocation applies during election campaigns and during other political campaigns such as political broadcasting prior to referenda. In *Wilson* v *IBA* (1979), a successful challenge was brought against the allocation of party political broadcast time prior to the Scottish devolution referendum. Allocation of time had been made to four political parties, three of which were campaigning in favour of the referendum proposals. The opponents of the referendum proposals argued successfully that they were being treated unfairly.

The European Court of Human Rights has taken a vigorous approach in protecting media comment on political ideas and politicians. A violation of Art 10 was held to have occurred in the case *Lingens* v *Austria* (1986). Lingens had published articles which contained strong criticism of Bruno Kreisky, the Austrian Chancellor. He had been found guilty of criminal defamation because he was unable to prove that his statements were true. The Court found that the interference with his right to freedom of expression was lawful and for a legitimate aim (the protection of the rights of others). However, the requirements for protection of the reputation of politicians have to be weighed in relation to the interest of open discussion of political issues. His comments concerned matters of opinion rather than fact. The criminal prosecution was disproportionate to the aim pursued and was therefore a violation of Art 10.

Incitement to racial or religious hatred

The Public Order Act 1986, s 17 provides that a person may not speak or act in a public place in a manner which is likely to engender racial hatred. An offence is committed by a person who, in a public place or at a public meeting, with the intention of stirring up hatred against a racial group in the United Kingdom, uses words or gestures which are threatening, abusive or insulting. It is also an offence to use threatening, abusive or insulting words or gestures in the knowledge that hatred against a racial group is likely to be stirred up. A racial group is defined as a group of persons defined by reference to colour, race, nationality or ethnic or national origins. Nationality in this context includes citizenship, so a racial group could consist of the members of a state with a multi-racial community. The Racial and Religious Hatred Act 2006 amended the provisions to include incitement to religious hatred. The provisions of the Public Order Act apply to written material, videos, films and sound tapes as well as to the original words or gestures. This restriction serves several purposes in the context of Art 10(2). It can protect public safety, prevent disorder, and protect the rights of others.

Discriminatory advertisements

Under the Sex Discrimination Act 1975, s 38, discriminatory advertise-
ments are unlawful. The use of job descriptions which might be taken
to indicate an intention to discriminate, and the use of job descriptions
with a sexual connotation such as "sales girl" or "barman" contravenes
the Act. A non-discrimination notice may be issued and an interdict may
be sought from the sheriff court to restrain a person from repeating the
unlawful act at any time within 5 years of a non-discrimination notice.
This restriction on the right to freedom of expression is for the purpose
of protecting the rights of others not to suffer discrimination.

Protecting the interests of national security

Official secrecy

Government information was protected until 1989 by the Official
Secrets Act 1911. Section 1 of that Act dealt largely with espionage and
is generally regarded as containing measures which are proportionate
to the legitimate aim in Art 10(2) of protecting national security.
Section 2, however, imposed a complete prohibition on the unauthorised
dissemination of official information, however trivial. Technically, it
was unlawful, for example, for a civil servant to tell someone what he
had for lunch. Section 2 became the subject of public criticism after
the prosecution of two civil servants during the 1980s for leaking
information which they felt was in the public interest. Sarah Tisdall
revealed that, contrary to official statements, American cruise missiles
had already arrived in the United Kingdom (*R* v *Tisdall* (1984)). Clive
Ponting provided information to Tam Dalyell MP which related to
the sinking of the Argentinian ship, the *Belgrano* (*R* v *Ponting* (1985)).
This finally led to a reform which was heralded as a big step towards
achieving openness in government but which in reality was not a radical
change. Section 2 of the Official Secrets Act 1911 was repealed and a
new Official Secrets Act was introduced in 1989. Section 1 of the 1911
Act is still available to punish spies.

The Official Secrets Act 1989 removed criminal sanctions for the
disclosure of some types of official information but it does not allow for
defences such as public interest, or prior disclosure or lack of *mens rea*,
and therefore introduces a stricter liability in relation to the categories
of information to which it applies. The Act applies to Ministers of the
Crown, civil servants, diplomats, police constables and members of the
armed forces. The following categories of information are protected by
the Act:

- information relating to security and intelligence;
- information relating to defence;
- information relating to international relations and any confidential information obtained from a state other than the United Kingdom or an international organisation;
- information, the disclosure of which results in, or is likely to result in, the commission of an offence, to facilitate escape from lawful custody, or to impede the prevention or detection of offences or the apprehension or prosecution of suspected offenders;
- any information obtained by reason of action taken under a warrant.

Not every disclosure of information will automatically amount to a criminal offence. In some cases it is necessary to prove that the disclosure was damaging. A disclosure relating to defence, for example, will be regarded as damaging if it reduces the capabilities of the armed forces, endangers life or equipment or endangers the interests of the United Kingdom, or of British citizens abroad, or is likely to have any of these effects. In the case *Lord Advocate* v *Scotsman Publications Ltd* (1989), which concerned the publication of a book by a former member of the intelligence and security services, the Lord Advocate claimed that the book contained information which was covered by the 1989 Act. It followed, therefore, that the author, Cavendish, was prohibited from disclosing it. The Crown had already conceded that the information was harmless. The court held that Cavendish was in breach of the Act but that when he circulated the memoirs to third parties, they did not commit an offence by disclosing harmless information. A third party would only be guilty of the offence if the information was damaging in the sense defined by the Act.

Some disclosures will be classed as criminal offences whether or not they are potentially damaging. Any disclosure by a member or former member of the security or intelligence services of information relating to security or intelligence is an offence, whether or not the disclosure is damaging (Official Secrets Act 1989, s 4). There can be no doubt that these restrictions are for legitimate purposes as defined by Art 10(2). Whether a prohibition of a disclosure which is not damaging is necessary in a democratic society is less certain.

Section 5 of the Act applies to persons other than Crown servants. Where a third party, such as a newspaper, has received information which was disclosed in contravention of the Official Secrets Act, it is not an offence merely to receive the information provided that it is not published. It is an offence, however, under s 8, to fail to comply with an official direction for the return or disposal of written information. Any subsequent disclosure by the third party will be an offence if it is made either knowing, or having reasonable cause to believe, that the information is protected under the Official Secrets Act. The maximum penalty for disclosing protected information is a period of imprisonment of up to 2 years, or a fine, or both.

There are defences to a prosecution under the Official Secrets Act. Where disclosure would only amount to an offence if it is damaging, it will be a defence to prove:

- that the accused did not know and had no reasonable cause to believe that disclosure would be damaging; or
- that the accused did not know and had no reasonable cause to suspect that the information disclosed related to one of the protected categories; or
- that he believed that he had lawful authority to disclose the information and had no reason to believe otherwise.

The Act contains no explicit public interest defence, so a person who has made a disclosure in order to reveal wrongdoing by public officials would have no defence. Alternative methods have been provided for a civil servant to pursue a grievance within their own department under civil service codes. Civil servants who wish to "blow the whistle" on illegal practices now share the same protection as other employees, under the Public Interest Disclosure Act 1998. In *R* v *Shayler* (2002) the defendant was charged with offences under s 1 of the Official Secrets Act. He argued that there should be a defence that the information which he disclosed was in the public interest. It was held that the defendant could have disclosed the information through civil service procedures, and so his freedom of expression was not restricted. The statutory requirement that there was no need to prove that a disclosure by a security service member was damaging was justified, since the lives of other secret service members could be put in danger, and the United Kingdom could be in breach of obligations under Arts 2 and 3.

Breach of confidence

Breach of confidence is a civil remedy which provides protection against the disclosure of information where the information has been entrusted to another. It is a remedy which is commonly used by commercial organisations but it may also be used by public authorities. In *Attorney-General* v *Jonathan Cape* (1976) the duty of confidentiality was effectively extended to "public" secrets and the Lord Chief Justice stated that the courts had jurisdiction to restrain publication of official information if it could be shown that the public interest demanded it. The civil law is more effective than criminal prosecutions for protecting public secrets for a number of reasons:

- the standard of proof is lower (balance of probabilities instead of the criminal standard of proof beyond reasonable doubt);
- there is no jury to sympathise with a public interest defence;
- civil actions can be brought to prevent publication whereas criminal prosecution can only be brought after the offence has been committed.

This does not mean that civil courts will always find in favour of restraining publication. There is a balance to be drawn between the interests of the government in protecting the information and the public interest in disclosure. The leading case in this area is *Attorney-General v Guardian Newspapers* (1990) in which it was held that publication is excusable where there is a serious and legitimate public interest in the information. Injunctions had been issued to prevent publications of extracts from the *Spycatcher* novel, which included allegations of illegal activity engaged in by MI5. The House of Lords decided that the public interest in knowing about the allegations in *Spycatcher* outweighed the interest in maintaining confidentiality. The fact that the novel had, by this time, been widely published outside the United Kingdom was also a material factor in this case. In *Lord Advocate v Scotsman Publications Ltd* (1989) the House of Lords upheld the refusal of interdicts against the publication of extracts from *Inside Intelligence* by Antony Cavendish. There had been prior publication of some of the materials and the risk of damage to national security was very remote. The *Observer* and the *Guardian* applied to the European Commission of Human Rights complaining about similar injunctions in England (*Observer and Guardian v United Kingdom* (1991)). The Court accepted that the injunctions had aims that were legitimate under Art 10(2) as they were deemed to be necessary in order to protect national security. However, the Court was not convinced that the injunctions were actually necessary for the whole period of time during which they had been applied. The injunctions ceased to be justified when the purpose was no longer to protect confidential information but rather to protect the reputation of the security service. Once the information was published outside the United Kingdom the injunctions were no longer necessary either to protect national security or to maintain the authority of the judiciary.

FREEDOM OF ASSEMBLY AND ASSOCIATION

Article 11 states:

> "1 Everyone has the right to freedom of peaceful assembly and to freedom of association with others, including the right to form and join trade unions for the protection of his interests.
>
> 2 No restrictions shall be placed on the exercise of these rights other than such as are prescribed by law and are necessary in a democratic society in the interests of national security or public safety, for the prevention of disorder or crime, for the protection of health or morals or for the protection of the rights and freedoms of others. This Article shall not prevent the imposition of lawful restrictions on the exercise of these rights by members of the armed forces, of the police or of the administration of the State."

The right to freedom of assembly and freedom of association is socially and culturally linked to the right to freedom of expression. The European Court of Human Rights has recognised the affinity between Art 11 and Art 10, referring to Art 11 as a specific application of the general principles of freedom of expression in Art 10 (*Ezelin* v *France* (1991)).

Article 11 protects two distinct types of activity:

- to meet with others as a group in public places;
- to become affiliated to organisations.

Article 11 specifies that this includes trade unions but other types of organisations are not excluded. The economic well-being of the country is not a legitimate aim in relation to Art 11, unlike Art 8. This Article only protects assemblies which are peaceful. There is no violation of the Article if the state regulates assemblies which are not peaceful or which are unlikely to be peaceful.

Positive obligation

Article 11 contains a positive obligation on states to protect the exercise of the rights contained therein. In *Plattform Ärzte für das Leben* v *Austria* (1988) it was held that the state had a duty to protect participants in a peaceful demonstration from interference by a violent group with opposing views. The Court held:

> "Genuine effective freedom of peaceful assembly cannot ... be reduced to a mere duty on the part of the State not to interfere: a purely negative conception would not be compatible with the

object and purpose of Article 11 ... Article 11 sometimes requires positive measures to be taken, even in the sphere of relations between individuals, if need be."

Freedom of assembly has always been regarded as an essential element in a society that claims to implement principles of civil and political freedom. The need for individuals to gather together in groups may be less important now that there are other means of communication such as television, telephones and the internet but two types of mass public meetings continue to be held:

- Public meetings are still important in industrial disputes where mass rallies and picketing of organisations are seen as a useful method of attracting publicity for a cause. During the miners' strike in the mid-1980s large numbers of pickets gathered at the steelworks at Ravenscraig and at Hunterston power station. The police diverted vehicles carrying pickets while they were some distance from either destination.

- Processions are still a popular way to attract the attention of the mass news media to a political or environmental cause. Certain traditional processions, such as marches by members of Orange Orders, still take place in parts of Scotland.

There are also other occasions when members of the public gather together in large groups. Examples include: gala days, fêtes and music festivals. There is also an increasing number of mass gatherings which take the form of a procession – examples include marathon races, common riding and charity walks. Any regulations which apply to assemblies and processions apply to such events.

Under Scots law, freedom of assembly exists only to the extent that people can assemble together in circumstances which are not subject to regulations or restrictions (*Aldred* v *Miller* (1925)). People may gather together in groups and may talk but the police could disperse them if they were obstructing the passage of others or if it was deemed likely that a breach of the peace may occur. The European Court of Human Rights considered the right to peaceful assembly in the case of *Ezelin* v *France* (1991). Ezelin was a lawyer who had taken part in a public demonstration. The demonstration started as a peaceful protest but became rowdy and some buildings were daubed with graffiti. The Public Prosecutor could not identify those responsible for the insulting behaviour or graffiti but he asked the Bar Council to take disciplinary action against Ezelin, who had remained at the scene, although he had not participated in the rowdy behaviour. He was sentenced to a formal reprimand which was upheld on appeal. The Court found that there was an interference with his right of peaceful assembly. The interference was in accordance with law and was for the legitimate aim of preventing disorder. However, the proportionality principle demands that a balance be struck between the requirements of the purposes listed in Art 11(2) and those of free expression by word, gesture or even silence by persons assembled on the streets or in other public places. The sanction was excessive and was therefore not necessary in a democratic society. This was the first case in which the Court found a breach of the right of peaceful assembly. The judgment does not distinguish between assemblies which take the form of protest marches and those which are static assemblies or rallies. The fact that the assembly as a whole ceased to be peaceful does not remove the protection from an individual whose actions did not overstep the boundaries of peaceful protest.

Where meetings are held on private property, the regulation of the meeting is a matter for the owner of the property. Many meetings are held on premises belonging to local authorities and local authorities have statutory duties to make premises available for political meetings in the period prior to an election. The law also takes steps to protect meetings from disruption by others. It is an offence for a person to attend a public meeting and to act in a disorderly manner for the purpose of impeding the business of the meeting. There is a specific sanction in relation to political meetings in the period leading up to elections. The Representation of the People Act 1983 provides that a person who, at a political meeting held in any constituency between the date of issue of a writ for the return of a Member of Parliament and the date of the election, acts or incites others to act in a disorderly manner for the purpose of disrupting the meeting shall be guilty of an illegal practice.

LEGITIMATE PURPOSES FOR INTERFERENCE WITH RIGHTS UNDER ART 11

The interest of public safety and the protection of public order

Public processions are regulated by the Civic Government (Scotland) Act 1982 (as amended by the Police, Public Order and Criminal Justice (Scotland) Act 2006) and the Public Order Act 1986 (as amended by the Criminal Justice and Public Order Act 1994). Local councils have the power to permit a procession to take place or to prohibit the holding of a procession. Twenty-eight-days' notice must be given prior to a procession taking place. Notice must be given to both the council and the chief constable. The requirement to give notice does not apply to funeral processions organised by a funeral director. Certain other types of marches or processions may be granted exemption from the need to give 28 days' notice in orders made by the Scottish Ministers. Such orders apply throughout Scotland, ensuring that the rules are consistent across Scotland. In certain circumstances, where processions are arranged in response to unforeseen events, the 28-day notification period may be waived.

When permission is given to hold a procession, the council may impose conditions as to its date, time, duration and route. It may also prohibit the procession from entering into any public place specified in the order. When deciding whether to prevent a march or place conditions on it, a local authority can consider the likely effect the march will have with regard to public safety, public order, damage to property and any disruption to the life of the community. Local authorities should also consider whether the march may place too much of a burden on the police. A council may, for example, prohibit a march by an Orange Order from entering a predominantly Catholic street. If a march is proposed which is the same or similar to a march held previously (for example, a yearly Orange Order march), a local authority, when considering whether to prevent the march or place conditions on it, can take account of:

- the effect of the previous march on public safety, public order, damage to property and any disruption to the life of the community;
- how far the previous march placed too much of a burden on police and other public services; and
- how far people taking part followed any code of conduct or guidance issued.

Appeal against a prohibition of a procession or any conditions imposed may be made to a sheriff, but only on the ground that the council has exceeded its powers. The sheriff may therefore uphold an appeal only if the council erred in law or based its decision on a material error of fact, or exercised its discretion unreasonably. The sheriff may not consider the merits of the decision, only whether the council was acting within its authority.

In *Aberdeen Bon-Accord Loyal Orange Lodge 701* v *Aberdeen City Council* (2001) the court was of the opinion that the council's reasons for its decision were not made out and an outright ban was disproportionate. The sheriff stated: "This right [under Article 11] is not restricted to those whose views accord with the majority. It is the essence of a civilised democratic society that many points of view may be expressed in public." The sheriff went on to indicate that the right to public assembly may be restricted but the action proposed needed to be proportionate to the risks which might arise and provide a reasonable response to the perceived risk. The sheriff considered that "a complete prohibition requires much more than a 'concern that the procession might promote religious intolerance and might interfere with the rights of other citizens to go about their business freely and lawfully' ... It is the right of individuals and groups in a civilised society to express their views as long as neither their words nor their actions contravene the law".

It is an offence to hold a procession without permission or to contravene the conditions which have been laid down. Any person who takes part in an unauthorised procession and who refuses to desist when ordered by a policeman in uniform is also guilty of an offence. The powers of a council relate mainly to regulating the holding of processions in advance of them taking place. Regulation of processions at the time when they are taking place falls within the powers of the police.

Requiring that permission be obtained before an assembly takes place or imposing conditions on an assembly will not necessarily amount to a contravention of Art 11 provided that the restrictions are imposed for a legitimate purpose. In the case of *Rassemblement Jurassien and Unité Jurassienne* v *Switzerland* (1979) the applicants were political organisations seeking independence for the Jura region. They organised a demonstration in the town of Moutier. An anti-separatist group organised a meeting in a restaurant in the town on the same day. The Council then banned all political meetings in the town for 2 days. The Commission stated that the ban in Moutier was for a very short duration and was not disproportionate. A longer ban on public processions was imposed in London in 1978 (*Christians against Racism and Fascism* v *United Kingdom* (1980)). The association of Christians against Racism and Fascism was an ecumenical Christian association which had been set up to oppose fascism and racist conduct. This was a time when the National Front was very active and there had been riots and disturbances resulting from several public processions by the National Front and counter-demonstrations by other organisations. The Metropolitan Police Commissioner decided to ban all public processions in London for 2 months. The Commission decided that it was not disproportionate for the authorities to issue the ban. The interference with the freedom of assembly must be balanced against the scale of the disorder which is likely to ensue if the assembly takes place.

The Public Order Act 1986 gives power to a senior police officer who is present when a procession is taking place to impose conditions if he reasonably believes that the procession may give rise to serious public disorder, serious damage to property or serious disruption to the life of the community, or that the purpose of the organisers is to intimidate others. Conditions may be imposed with regard to the time, place and manner of the procession but only in so far as they are necessary to prevent serious disorder, disruption or intimidation. It is an offence to knowingly fail to comply with conditions imposed by the police on the day of a procession or to incite others to behave in a manner contrary to the conditions. It is a defence for a person to prove that the failure to comply with the conditions arose from circumstances outwith his control.

Regulation of assemblies

Similar powers to those by which the police regulate processions are conferred on the police in relation to other public assemblies. These would include political protests, picketing in the course of an industrial dispute, and social occasions. The police officer may make conditions regarding the location of the assembly, the duration and the maximum number of people who may attend. As with processions, the conditions imposed must not be more stringent than is required to prevent serious disorder, damage to property or disruption. A public assembly is defined as 20 or more persons gathered in a public place which is wholly or partly open to the air. A public place means any road and any place to which the public has access. A person who knowingly fails to comply with the directions of the police or who incites others to disregard the conditions is guilty of an offence. Conditions may also be imposed in advance by the chief constable. Written notice of the conditions must be given to the organisers of the assembly.

Trespassory assemblies are prohibited. A trespassory assembly is where 20 or more people assemble on land entirely in the open air, to which the public has no right of access or only limited right of access. If a chief constable reasonably believes that a trespassory assembly is about to take place and that it is likely to cause serious disruption to the life of the community or significant damage to the land or a building or a monument on it, he may apply to the local authority for an order prohibiting all trespassory assemblies for a period of up to 4 days in an area not exceeding a radius of 5 miles from the intended location of the assembly. This power applies where the land, building or monument is of historical, architectural, archaeological or scientific importance. Examples include Stonehenge at the time of the summer solstice and areas around Faslane naval base. Any person who organises or takes part in an assembly which trespasses onto land in the area for which a prohibition order is in effect commits a criminal offence. A uniformed police officer is entitled to stop a person whom he reasonably believes to be on his way to an assembly which has been prohibited. The police officer can direct him not to proceed in the direction of the assembly and failure to comply with the instructions of the police officer is an offence.

Indirect restrictions on the right of assembly

Obstruction of the highway The Civic Government (Scotland) Act 1982 provides that any person who, in a public place:

- obstructs, along with another or others, the lawful passage of any other person and fails to desist on being required to do so by a constable in uniform; or
- wilfully obstructs the lawful passage of any other person,

is guilty of an offence.

It is not necessary for a street or footpath to be completely blocked in order for the highway to be regarded as obstructed. It may be classed as obstruction if there is still room for people to pass by. People could, in theory, be charged with the offence of obstruction if they gathered in a road for a few minutes and caused only a short delay to people wishing to use the road.

Obstruction of a police officer It is an offence to obstruct a police officer in the execution of his duty. Prosecutions for the obstruction of a police officer are not common. It is more usual for a person who has acted in a manner which impedes the work of a police officer to be charged with breach of the peace.

Breach of the peace The all-encompassing common law offence of breach of the peace provides the grounds on which the police may prevent and control any public disorder. It is not necessary for a breach of the peace to have occurred before a public assembly is dispersed or individual participants are apprehended. It is sufficient for there to be, in the opinion of the police, a reasonable probability that a breach of the peace may occur.

It is not necessary to prove that an individual accused person was acting in breach of the peace. A person may be convicted of breach of the peace if he was part of a crowd of people acting in a disorderly manner and he did not disassociate himself from the crowd. In the case of *Winnik* v *Allan* (1986), the conviction was upheld of a man who had been part of a crowd of noisy and disorderly persons who shouted and swore and tore down a stone boundary wall and threw missiles at colliery buildings. His actions had not been singled out in the evidence at his trial but the evidence of the behaviour of the group was sufficient to give rise to the inference that he had supported, sympathised with and encouraged the actions of the crowd.

This power to intervene is not restricted to assemblies held in public places. The police are also entitled to attend where a public meeting is being held on private premises. They can do so if they have reasonable grounds for believing that an offence such as a breach of the peace is imminent or even that there is a strong probability that there may be a breach of the peace.

Football banning orders   Under the Police, Public Order and Criminal Justice (Scotland) Act 2006, a court may impose a football banning order on an individual convicted of an offence, instead of or in addition to any sentence the court could impose for the offence. The court must be satisfied that the offence involved engaging in violence or disorder and that it related to a football match. The court must also be satisfied that there are reasonable grounds to believe that making the order would help to prevent violence or disorder at or in connection with any football matches.

FREEDOM OF ASSOCIATION

The rights which Art 11 confers, to join or to refrain from joining an organisation, do not necessarily apply to every type of association. In *Chassagnou* v *France* (1999) the Court stated that the term "association" has an autonomous meaning in the context of the Convention. Whether an association falls within the ambit of Art 11 does not depend upon the way in which it has been classified under national law, so, for example, organisations such as professional regulatory bodies may not fall within the scope of Art 11 although trade associations such as federations of taxi drivers do fall within its remit. The right to form and join trade unions includes the right to choose not to join a trade union. In *Young,*

James and Webster v *United Kingdom* (1981), the applicants complained that their rights had been infringed when they were dismissed from their jobs for refusing to join a trade union. Their employer had agreed to employ only union members. This was known as a "closed shop". Under employment law at that time their dismissals were deemed to be fair and so they had no right to compensation. The Court held that, although the interference with their rights under Art 11 was in accordance with the law and had the legitimate purpose of being for the protection of the rights and freedoms of others, it was not necessary in a democratic society as the detriment to the individuals was not justified by the overall benefits to society.

Deprivation of the right to join a trade union was considered in the case of *Council of Civil Service Unions* v *United Kingdom* (1988). It was held that a ban on union membership at Government Communications Headquarters was justified in the interests of national security. The Commission found that, although there had been interference with the rights under Art 11(1), in terms of Art 11(2), the applicants fell into the category of members of the administration of the state and therefore the imposition of lawful restrictions on the exercise of these rights is specifically allowed. The Commission decided that the second sentence in Art 11(2) did not require that the interference should be necessary in a democratic society and the application was, therefore, declared inadmissible. (This provision is only found in Art 11.)

A law which compels a person to join an association which is fundamentally contrary to his own opinions and beliefs may constitute an infringement of Art 11 (*Chassagnou* v *France* (1999)). Chassagnou was the owner of a small plot of land. He was opposed to hunting on ethical grounds but he was required under French national law to join an approved hunters' association and to allow its members to hunt on his land. It was held that there was a breach of Art 11, since to force a person to join an association contrary to his own beliefs and to surrender his land to a use of which he disapproved went beyond what was necessary to protect the democratic participation in hunting.

In relation to the United Kingdom, the restrictions on the political activities of local government officers came under scrutiny in the case of *Ahmed* v *United Kingdom* (2000). Local government officers holding "politically restricted posts" could not participate in political activities. *Ahmed* applied to the European Court of Human Rights, on the ground that the regulations breached Art 11. It was held that the regulations pursued the legitimate aim of protecting the rights of both council members and the electorate to effective local political democracy, which required political neutrality on the part of officers. Furthermore, the regulations were "necessary in a democratic society", since they had been introduced as a result of a pressing social need to reduce the risk of abuse of power by local government officers. It was held by a majority that there had been no violation of Art 11.

Frequently Asked Questions

Is a remedy granted once it has been proved that there has been interference with a Convention right?

No. Misconceptions about this point in press articles were the cause of a public opinion to the effect that the Human Rights Act 1998 is a charter for criminals. Proving that a right has been infringed is only the first stage of considering a case. The court then goes on to consider whether the infringement was according to law, for a legitimate purpose and necessary in a democratic society. A remedy is granted only if one of these conditions is not met.

Is freedom of expression under Art 10 more important than the right of privacy under Art 8?

Freedom of expression is regarded as a fundamental requirement in a democracy and freedom of expression has been afforded special status under the Human Rights Act 1998. However, this does not mean that it will always take precedence over other rights. Each case must be considered carefully and the rights of one party balanced against the rights of the other.

Why is the law relating to marches and processions stricter now than it was prior to the Human Rights Act 1998?

Recent changes in the law have increased the period of notice which must be given to a local council and to the police, from 7 days to 28 days. The principle that processions which have been customarily held are exempt from the need to apply for permission no longer applies. The changes in the law give councils more power to impose conditions on processions. They are allowed to take into account information about problems which occurred the previous time a procession was held. Orange Lodge parades have caused particular public order problems in the past and the new rules will give councils more scope to ensure, for example, that such parades are not routed in a way that will cause offence to others.

Essential Facts

- Qualified rights are the right to respect for private and family life, one's home and correspondence, the right to freedom of thought, conscience and religion, to freedom of expression and to freedom of assembly and association.

- Qualified rights are expressed in two parts: the first part defines the right conferred on the individual and the second part sets out the public interest matters which would amount to a legitimate purpose for the state to restrict the right.

- The right to private and family life relates to a wider concept than "family". It includes business or professional activities. It also includes the right to live in a manner suited to one's own personal beliefs and inclinations.

- A state may be in contravention of Art 8 if it does not provide adequate legal safeguards to protect the privacy of individuals through measures such as data protection legislation.

- Scots law does not recognise a right of privacy *per se*.

- Interception of communications is permitted only where there is a clear legal authority.

- Interference with correspondence between a prisoner and a lawyer is contrary to Art 8.

- Freedom of thought, conscience and religion includes the right to manifest the belief by, for example, attending religious services, or by expressing opinions.

- The courts must balance carefully the rights of one person under Arts 8 or 9 (privacy, or religion or belief) against the rights of others under Art 10 (freedom of expression) as there will often be competing interests.

- Freedom of assembly concerns rights to protest and to meet in public places. Freedom of association concerns rights to join organisations, societies, trade unions, etc.

• Permission from the local council is required in order for processions and assemblies to be held lawfully. Unlawful assemblies may be dispersed by the police.

Essential Cases

Douglas v Hello! Ltd (2001): privacy – Michael Douglas's wedding.

Mosley v News Group (2008): privacy – public interest in sexual activities of celebrity.

Campbell v Mirror Group Newspapers (2004): – privacy – supermodel Naomi Campbell – drugs.

Smith v United Kingdom (1999): intrusions by military authorities into private lives.

Ahmed, Petitioner (2000): right to family life not infringed by immigration and deportation rules.

Malone v United Kingdom (1984): interception of communications without lawful authority is a breach of Art 8.

Halford v United Kingdom (1997): intercepting phone calls on private premises with no advance warning breached Art 8.

Campbell v United Kingdom (1992): interference with correspondence between a prisoner and a lawyer is contrary to Art 8.

Handyside v United Kingdom (1976): obscene publications – margin of appreciation.

Lord Advocate v Scotsman Publications Ltd (1989): Cavendish papers – official secrecy.

Attorney-General v Guardian Newspapers (1990): *Spycatcher* novel – breach of confidence.

Ezelin v France (1991): key principles of freedom of assembly.

Council of Civil Service Unions v United Kingdom (1988): right to join a trade union could be restricted in the interests of national security.

6 OTHER RIGHTS

There are some substantive rights which do not fall into the categories of fundamental, procedural or qualified rights. They are collected here for convenience.

They are:

- right to marry and found a family (Art 12);
- freedom from discrimination (Art 14);★
- right to peaceful enjoyment of possessions (First Protocol, Art 1);
- right to education (First Protocol, Art 2);
- right to free elections (First Protocol, Art 3).

RIGHT TO MARRY AND FOUND A FAMILY

Article 12 states:

> "Men and women of marriageable age have the right to marry and to found a family, according to the national laws governing the exercise of this right."

This Article recognises that states may have different laws relating to capacity to marry and the formalities which may be required. The right to marry and to found a family does not confer a right to end a marriage by divorce. In *Johnston* v *Ireland* (1987) an applicant claimed that his right to marry and found a family was violated by Irish law, which prevented him divorcing his first wife and marrying the woman with whom he lived. Prisoners are entitled to marry but the right to marry need not extend to the right to conjugal visits while in prison (*X* v *United Kingdom* (1975)).

The right of to marry was not extended transsexuals in the United Kingdom until recently. In *Goodwin* v *United Kingdom* (2002) a male-to-female transsexual complained that the United Kingdom was in breach of Art 12 by not allowing her to register as a woman and by confining lawful marriage to a couple born respectively male and female. The European Court of Human Rights held that there was no justification for a bar to the marriage of transsexuals in their acquired gender. The law in the United

---

★ Article 14 is not a stand-alone right. It is applicable only when a claim is made for the infringement of another substantive right.

Kingdom has now developed and, under the Civil Partnerships Act 2004, same-sex couples can obtain legal recognition of their relationship by forming a civil partnership. They may do so by registering as civil partners of each other provided:

- they are of the same sex;
- they are not already in a civil partnership or lawfully married;
- they are not within the prohibited degrees of relationship;
- they are both aged 16 or over.

FREEDOM FROM DISCRIMINATION

Article 14 states:

> "The enjoyment of rights and freedoms set forth in this Convention shall be secured without discrimination on any ground such as sex, race, colour, language, religion, political or other opinion, national or social origin, association with a national minority, property, birth or other status."

Article 14 does not give protection against discrimination *per se*. It gives protection against discrimination only in connection with other Convention rights. Article 14 therefore has no independent existence. A measure which is otherwise in conformity with the Convention may amount to a violation of Art 14 if it is of a discriminatory nature. The principle of equality of treatment is violated if any distinction on grounds of sex, race, colour, language, religion, political or other opinion, national or social origin, association with a national minority, property, birth or status has no objective and reasonable justification.

Often when claims are made to the European Court of Human Rights which include a contention that there has been a breach of Art 14, the issue of discrimination under Art 14 is not considered. This is because it is not deemed to be necessary to deliberate on the issue of differential treatment if the Court finds that there has been a breach of another substantive right. This approach was explained in the case of *Dudgeon* v *United Kingdom* (1982) wherein it was stated:

> "Where a substantive Article of the Convention has been invoked both on its own and together with Article 14 and a separate breach has been found of the substantive Article, it is not generally necessary for the Court also to examine the case under Article 14, though the position is otherwise if a clear inequality of treatment in the enjoyment of the right in question is a fundamental aspect of the case."

There is no need to establish that another right has been breached for a remedy under Art 14 to be granted. There have been many occasions when the European Court of Human Rights has found that there has not been a breach of the Article which is the main substance of the application but has awarded a remedy for discriminatory treatment under Art 14. In the case of *Abdulaziz, Cabales and Balkandali* v *United Kingdom* (1985) it was held that the immigration rules for entry into the United Kingdom were in violation of Art 14. Under the regulations it was easier for the wives of men residing in the United Kingdom to enter than it was for the husbands of wives residing in the United Kingdom. The applicants were women who claimed that this amounted to a breach of Art 8, the right to family life, and to a breach of Art 14. The Government argued that the difference in treatment between men and women was justified on the basis that immigration of men needed to be more tightly controlled in order to protect the domestic labour market. The Court held that the rules were not incompatible with Art 8, but Art 14 had been violated by the difference in treatment accorded to men and women. The rules were amended as a result of the case.

Despite the straightforward wording of Art 14, applying it to a factual situation is a matter of some complexity. In recent cases in the United Kingdom, the courts have adopted a structured approach based on a series of questions to be answered. This approach was followed by the House of Lords in *R (on the application of S)* v *Chief Constable of South Yorkshire* (2004). The questions were as follows:

1 Do the facts fall within the ambit of one or more of the Convention rights?
2 Was there a difference of treatment in respect of that right between the claimant and others put forward for comparison?
3 If so, was the difference in treatment on one or more of the proscribed grounds under Art 14?
4 Were those others in an analogous situation?
5 Was the difference in treatment objectively justifiable in the sense that it had a legitimate aim and bore a reasonable relationship or proportionality to that aim?

These questions are useful but it is still difficult, for example, to decide whether other people were in a truly analogous situation. The similarity of circumstances must relate to relevant matters but the circumstances do not have to be identical. The key question is whether a difference in treatment between one person and another was justified.

The case of *A* v *Secretary of State for the Home Department* (2004) was a challenge to provisions of the Anti-terrorism, Crime and Security Act 2001 under which foreign nationals suspected of terrorism offences could be imprisoned indefinitely but British suspects could not. The possibility of indefinite imprisonment was claimed to be a breach of Art 5 and the difference in treatment for British subjects and foreign nationals was claimed to breach Art 14. The two groups of suspects were in an analogous situation and the difference in treatment could not be justified.

Article 14 does no more than provide a guarantee that people will not receive different treatment because of their sex, race, colour, language, religion, political or other opinion, national or social origin, association with a national minority, property, birth or status. It does not create a positive obligation on a state to preserve the culture and language of minority groups. In the *Belgian Linguistic case (No 2)* (1979–80) the Court held that Art 14 does not guarantee to a parent or to a child the right to receive instruction in the language of his choice. The obligation under Art 14 is to ensure that the right to education shall be secured to everyone within its jurisdiction, without discrimination on the ground, for instance, of language.

Protocol 12 to the Convention is intended to replace Art 14 with a stand-alone prohibition against discrimination which would create a positive duty on a state to protect people within the jurisdiction from discrimination on the same grounds as those listed in Art 14. The United Kingdom has not ratified Protocol 12. The preferred approach in the United Kingdom is to legislate against specific types of discrimination.

PROTECTION OF PROPERTY

Article 1 of Protocol 1 states:

> "Every natural or legal person is entitled to the peaceful enjoyment of his possessions. No one shall be deprived of his possessions except in the public interest and subject to the conditions provided for by law and by the general principles of international law.
>
> The preceding provisions shall not, however, in any way impair the right of a State to enforce such laws as it deems necessary to control the use of property in accordance with the general interest or to secure the payment of taxes or other contributions or penalties."

The Human Rights Act 1998 also gives further effect to the rights contained in Protocol 1 to the European Convention on Human Rights with the result that Protocol 1 rights must also be taken into account by UK courts.

Article 1, although not usually included in the category of a qualified right, operates in a similar way. First of all it sets out a general principle conferring a right of peaceful enjoyment of possessions. It then goes on to specify two sets of circumstance in which the state can interfere with the right of peaceful enjoyment:

- deprivation of property by the state is allowed if it is in the public interest.
- a state can control the use of property in accordance with the general interest or to secure the payment of taxes or other contributions or penalties.

In *Sporrong and Lonnroth* v *Sweden* (1983), the applicants owned land in Stockholm. Plans for development were proposed and expropriation permits were signed by the Government. The notices would mean that properties would be purchased by the Government when the development was due to start. The local administration board then issued notices prohibiting any construction on the land. The expropriation permits lasted 23 years and the prohibition notices lasted for 25 years. In the meantime the owners of property could not build on their land and were not entitled to compensation. It was held that there was a violation of Art 1 as the state had not exercised its rights in accordance with the overall principle of allowing peaceful enjoyment of possessions.

"Possessions" are not confined to land and buildings, furniture, jewellery, cash or stocks and shares. The word has an autonomous meaning under the Convention and includes a variety of economic interests such as patents, planning consents and, in some circumstances, money.

Deprivation of possession subject to conditions

The principle that the deprivation must be lawful has the same meaning as similar provisions elsewhere in the Convention. This means that to be lawful the restriction must:

- have an established legal basis in domestic law, such as legislation;
- be accessible to those affected;
- be foreseeable.

The restriction must be sufficiently clear so that those affected can understand it and act accordingly.

Temporary interference may not be a deprivation. In *Air Canada* v *United Kingdom* (1995) the temporary seizure of an aircraft to enforce specific provisions in drugs legislation was held not to be a violation of Art 1. The aircraft had been seized and then returned after a payment had been made. It was held to be a proportionate way to encourage Air Canada to improve security.

Where a deprivation of property has occurred, principles of fairness require that compensation should be paid. In *Lithgow* v *United Kingdom* (1986) the owners of aircraft and shipping companies which had been nationalised in 1977 complained that they had not received proper compensation. It was held that the Court will respect the national legislature's judgment with respect to compensation schemes unless they are manifestly unfair. This reflects the wide margin of appreciation which is afforded with regard to deprivation and control of property.

Control of property

The right to control property in the general interest includes such matters as planning controls designed to protect nature, or maintain a green belt, or to protect the environment. In *Chapman* v *United Kingdom* (2001), the applicant was a gypsy who wanted to live in a caravan on land that she owned but the local authority refused to give her planning permission. It was held that her wish to live on the land had to be weighed against the objections which had been made on environmental grounds. The interference with her enjoyment of the property was proportionate and fairly balanced against the requirements of Art 1.

Although there is an accepted entitlement to compensation when there is deprivation of property, there may not be such a right when property is merely controlled. In *R* v *Secretary of State for Health, ex parte Eastside Cheese Co* (1999), an emergency control order was made under the Food Safety Act 1990 to prevent the use of certain cheeses by a manufacturer. It was held that the company had not been deprived of the property and compensation was not required.

Interferences with rights under Art 1

General interest

The concept of "general interest" is very wide but it is taken to include the legitimate purposes for which other qualified rights may be restricted by the state.

Prevention of crime

Since the 1980s, there have been laws in place in Scotland to enable property which has been used in a crime, or property which can be identified as proceeds of a crime, to be confiscated. Originally there were separate provisions for certain types of crime but the law is now contained in the Proceeds of Crime Act 2002. The Act applies throughout the United Kingdom so that property gained by criminal activity in one jurisdiction cannot be hidden in another. The Act establishes the Assets Recovery Agency, which is responsible for the operation of the confiscation regime. It includes legal safeguards, such as a right of appeal.

Prevention of the spread of a disease

In *Westerhall Farm* v *Scottish Ministers* (2001), the livestock of a farm was ordered to be culled during an outbreak of foot and mouth disease. The farm was within 3 km of a case of foot and mouth disease so all cattle had to be slaughtered. The petitioner argued that the policy was inflexible and disproportionate but it was held that the requirement for swift and effective action rendered the actions of the Scottish Ministers proportionate.

General economic well-being of the country

In *R (on the application of Denson)* v *Child Support Agency* (2002) the claimant argued that the actions of the Child Support Agency in forcing him to pay maintenance for his children under the Child Support Act 1991 were in breach of Art 1. It was held that it was in the interest of the general community that the state should be able to recover maintenance payments from absent parents and reduce the burden on the taxpayer.

RIGHT TO EDUCATION

Article 2 of the First Protocol states:

> "No person shall be denied the right to education. In the exercise of any functions which it assumes in relation to education and to teaching, the State shall respect the right of parents to ensure such education and teaching in conformity with their own religious and philosophical convictions."

The United Kingdom entered a reservation to Art 2 of the Protocol in March 1952, confining compliance to compatibility with "the provision of efficient instruction and training, and the avoidance of unreasonable expenditure". Unlike derogations, reservations such as this one do not cease to have effect after 5 years. In *Costello-Roberts* v *United Kingdom* (1995) the European Court of Human Rights held that, even if a state is not itself the education provider whose decision is being challenged, it is the state's duty under Art 11, to secure the right to education to everyone in its jurisdiction. The right to education must be guaranteed equally to children in private and state schools.

In the case of *Campbell and Cosans* v *United Kingdom* (1982), two mothers claimed that the use of corporal punishment in Scottish schools was a violation of Art 2. The Court rejected the argument that the use of the tawse was inhuman and degrading but accepted that there was a violation of Art 2. The method of punishment used in a school could be an integral part of the school's ethos and so the parents could object to the use of corporal punishment on philosophical grounds. Philosophical convictions were defined by the Court as "such convictions as are worthy of respect in a democratic society" and which are "compatible with human dignity and which do not conflict with the right of the child to education". The United Kingdom pleaded in defence that the use of corporal punishment was necessary in order to provide efficient instruction and training and to avoid unreasonable expenditure on other forms of discipline. These arguments were not accepted. The Court held that a system of exemptions from corporal punishment would not conflict with efficient instruction. The use of corporal punishment in all state schools was abolished by the Education (No 2) Act 1986.

Suspending or excluding a child from school will not breach the Convention provided that:

- the expulsion must not prevent education being given elsewhere;
- it must not breach another Convention right, such as Art 6.

In Scotland a child under the age of 16 who is excluded from school has the right to appeal against the exclusion. The Standards in Scotland's Schools etc (Scotland) Act 2000, s 41, states that if a child is 12 years old or older it is presumed that he is of "sufficient age and maturity to have understanding" to instruct a solicitor to represent him. Failing this, the parent could appeal on his behalf.

RIGHT TO FREE ELECTIONS

Article 3 of the First Protocol states that:

"The High Contracting Parties undertake to hold free elections at reasonable intervals by secret ballot, under conditions which will ensure the free expression of the opinion of the people in the choice of legislature."

The rights conferred by this Article are not absolute and the states have a wide margin of appreciation in setting conditions for election provided that the conditions set do not limit the rights to such an extent as to undermine the basic principle of free elections. In *Hirst* v *United Kingdom* (2004) it was held that the UK law that all convicted prisoners were denied the right to vote was incompatible with the right to vote under the First Protocol to the Convention.

Frequently Asked Question

Are the groups of people protected from discrimination under Art 14 the same as those protected under UK discrimination laws?

No. UK discrimination laws protect on the grounds of race, sex, marital status, religion, sexual orientation, age and disability. Article 14 protects from discrimination on grounds of sex, race, colour, language, religion, political or other opinion, national or social origin, association with a national minority, property, birth or status. This is a much wider range of grounds. The scope of these grounds has been the subject of a number of cases and is still open to interpretation. For, example, birth or status has been held to apply in cases of discrimination against illegitimate children.

Essential Facts

- Article 14 (freedom from discrimination), is not a stand-alone right. It is applicable only when a claim is made for the infringement of another substantive right.
- The UK has not ratified Protocol 12, which would give a free-standing right to freedom from discrimination.
- Compensation is paid when there is a deprivation of property but not normally when property is only controlled.
- The UK entered a reservation to the right to education – restricting the right to avoid unreasonable expenditure.

Essential Cases

Johnston v Ireland (1987): no right to divorce.

Abdulaziz, Cabales and Balkandali v United Kingdom (1985): discrimination against women in immigration rules was unlawful.

R (on the application of S) v Chief Constable of South Yorkshire (2004): test for judging whether there has been discrimination.

A v Secretary of State for the Home Department (2004) (Belmarsh case): discrimination against foreign nationals.

R v Secretary of State for Health, ex parte Eastside Cheese Co (1999): compensation may not be due where property is only controlled and the owner has not been deprived of it.

Westerhall Farm v Scottish Ministers (2001): deprivation of property – foot and mouth disease.

Costello-Roberts v United Kingdom (1995); right to education applies to private as well as state schools.

Campbell and Cosans v United Kingdom (1982): right of parents to have education according to their philosophy, ie no corporal punishment.

Hirst v United Kingdom (2004): convicted prisoners – right to vote.

INDEX

Printed and bound by CPI Group (UK) Ltd, Croydon, CR0 4YY

31/12/2024

01813282-0004